# Her Price: Not Negotiable

by

## Panebi C. Smith

*Compliments of the Author*

authorHOUSE™

*1663 Liberty Drive, Suite 200*
*Bloomington, Indiana 47403*
*(800) 839-8640*
*www.AuthorHouse.com*

© *2004 Panebi C. Smith*
*All Rights Reserved.*

*No part of this book may be reproduced, stored in a retrieval system, or transmitted by any means without the written permission of the author.*

*First published by AuthorHouse 08/26/05*

*ISBN: 1-4208-0060-4(sc)*

*Library of Congress Control Number: 2004097185*

*Printed in the United States of America*
*Bloomington, Indiana*

*This book is printed on acid-free paper.*

# ACKNOWLEDGEMENTS

With gratitude to God, I wish to express my profound appreciation for the invaluable quota contributed to my life and worth by these precious and eternally relevant people of God.

***To My Father in the LORD, Rev. Dr. Emmanuel Olubayo Folarin. An Uncommon man of God with an uncommon impact and touch.*** A Father who gave me feather to soar to heights of eternal impact in the making of a life dedicated to the purpose and will of God. Through his leadership, my credibility as a witness to God's power and love has been built. Your reward is sure, eternal in the heavens.

Impeccably to Rev. Moses O. Fasanya, an Uncommon Mentor and God's answer to my quest for relevance and search for purpose. He did not give a dream but fine-tuned my God-given dream .God put the dial in his hands to fine tune my dream to divine frequency and give it clarity and colour. God used him to develop the film of my life, photographically speaking. You are remembered forever and your seed is blessed after you.

Special thanks goes to Eteimere Patience Toun, my cousin and a dear daughter of virtue to the family of Elder (Gen.) P.A.Toun. You believed in my dream and have been a witness to my testimony and credibility. You're blessed and remembered.

Also to Bukola Fasanya, (nee Ekundayo) a witness to my impact and in whom the character of a virtuous woman is personified. I treasure your episode in my life.

To God's daughters of virtue who, in my life's episodes, has had a feel of my impact including Elo Ofere, Elohor Onoriede, Efe Flora Irivbogbe, Miebi Jessica Aputu, my cousin, Augusta Ozinegbe, to mention but a few.

To Josephine Tamuno Ihuegbu, your love and purity inspired me in the making of this book. Your price is not negotiable. Keep the flame burning; and remain pure and undefiled. And to **Apostle Francis Ekundayo Okhiria**, of the Glorious Morning Star

Assembly, Brooklyn, New York, who was a Word made flesh to me when I immigrated to the United States. A man whose credibility and witness has been proved by divine approval. His integrity I greatly appreciate.

And to the two olive trees God planted around me when I sprouted as a tender plant and as a root out of a dry ground. To be nourished from their taproot, deeply embedded in the Word, in the persons of Revs.J.O.Doroh and Sunday Umukoro. And to Pastor Nelson Luckie Ogbemudia of Family Worship Centre, Abuja, Nigeria; a friend that sticks closer than a brother. Who discovered the seed in me and became *a word made flesh* to my life, calling out the best in me by the power of appreciation. To Bulus Musa, a Chartered Accountant, my beloved brother, friend and inspiration in Christ.

To my eldest sister, **Mrs Justina Olayemi**, nee Smith, who stood by me in encouragement and support at all times. You are loved and remembered.

Finally to my parents, **Mr. & Mrs. Smith Mission Orukari**, who gave me my form and definition; Especially my mum, Grace Smith, her virtue is a coat of many colours and I pray it reproduced in my wife to come.

# DEDICATION.

My heart overflows with joy and my spirit resounds with praise and thanksgiving as I dedicate this book to God, the most High and Almighty, the Fountain of Wisdom *whose* **Everlasting Arms** bear the weight of His creation, you and I inclusive; *whose* **Omnipresent Eye** maintains equilibrium in the universe, *whose* **Omniscient Mind** knows the pains we bear and willing to share, with an **Omnipotent Assurance** that we are not alone in our earthly sojourn and cannot be left alone. To Him I give my unconditional love and eternal gratitude.

Also, to the **Girl of my Dreams.** Her price is not negotiable!

# Table of Contents

ACKNOWLEDGEMENTS ................................................................ iii

DEDICATION. ............................................................................... v

FOREWORD ............................................................................... vii

GIRL OF MY DREAMS. ............................................................ viii

INTRODUCTION ......................................................................... x

HER BODY: The Force of Relativity ............................................ 1

HER NAKEDNESS: The Beauty of Suspense ............................ 21

HER VIRGINITY: The Priceless Gift of Bonding ...................... 31

HER SEXUALITY: The Fountain of Nourishment ..................... 43

HER LOVE: The Unconditional Choice ..................................... 65

HER PASSION: The Spring of Inspiration .................................. 87

HER BEAUTY: The Inner Source of Strength .......................... 106

HER VIRTUE: The Divine Endowment .................................... 125

HER GROWTH: The Power of Appreciation ........................... 137

HER PAST: The Grace of Redemption ..................................... 151

HER FULFILLMENT: The Purpose of Creation ...................... 162

Epilogue: ANSWERS FROM THE FATHER'S HEART ........... 186

# FOREWORD

At every point in time, God inspires people to write for the benefit of humanity.

Brother Churchill Smith, out of his inward vision, has received inspiration, which he has been able to translate into revelation. This revelation has led to the putting into black and white eleven chapters of a book titled "Her Price: Not Negotiable."

The focus of this book is on the female sex, but he has been able to translate what ordinarily looks carnal to many believers into having a profound relationship with God's design and purpose for His female creation.

The expositions given on chapters like **her sexuality, her love, her passion and her beauty** are quite revealing and helpful to both adult and youth.

**"Her Sexuality: The Fountain of Nourishment"**, coming from a youth is quite impressive. This book in summary is a bold step at digging into the Holy Scriptures and proving that the female creation is not evil in her making but the understanding of the vessel herself either brings good or evil.

I recommend this book to both adults and youths and to all who want to know and understand the female creation of God.

**Rev.Dr. (Mrs) F.E.Folarin**
**Senior Pastor, Divine Christian Assembly**
**Agric, Ojo**
**Lagos-Nigeria.**

# GIRL OF MY DREAMS.

There is a dream incubated in every man's heart regardless colour, creed, race or calling, arising from an innate need. An obvious vacuum that despite status or standing longs to be filled: The quest for a woman.

Every man needs praise, one to cheer him on the job and accord him due regards. He needs assurance that he would succeed in his mission. He needs nourishment and food, beyond the edible, soul provender. Man needs support, a companion to stand by him and compliment his function. Man needs a healer, of his bruised and battered ego; one to revive his fighting spirit and remind him that he was born to conquer, to dominate, to take charge and subdue. That the earth is his parish and, like the eagle, he was made for the heights, born for heavenly adventures.

Man needs a reward; to see his conquest and prowess reproduced in his seed and occupying his conquered territory. Man needs an answer from God to contain the mystery of companionship and relativity and the woman became God's answer.

All though my years, I have carried and nursed this dream, being fine-tuned by God's word and discipline. Locked up within me, in the subterranean chambers of my being, and flowing like molten lava spilling over in strangely moving language, is a river of poetry and worship of the deep mysteries of God in the making and relativity of the Woman. I have not reduced my quest to manageable proportions rather; I float on the waves and enter into the mystery of it through poetry. Responding with poetic rhythm and praise. Indeed some of my finest poems have been inspired from godly and productive fellowship with some of God's daughters of virtue.

This book was borne from an inspiration of one of such friends. A fraction of the divine purpose for her life was what God gave me shortly after we became acquainted.

God told me she has got a price; that she is empowered with divine presence and endowed with His essence which gives her a price and that her price is not negotiable. It must be fully paid, relatively and absolutely, to meet her fulfilment. Everything about her goes to make up that price.

**Her Body**: the force of relativity: **Her Nakedness:** the beauty of suspense to one man; **Her Virginity:** the priceless gift of bonding her to one man; **Her Sexuality:** the fountain of nourishment to one man; **Her Love:** the unconditional choice in loving one man; **Her Passion:** the spring of inspiration in creating your man's world; **Her Beauty:** the inner source of strength; **Her Virtue:** the divine endowment; **Her Growth:** the power of appreciation; **Her Past:** the grace of redemption in the blood of Jesus, the Seed of the woman; **Her Fulfilment:** the purpose of creation. Talking about her, *good things are properly stored and when they are exhibited they are protected.*

She is a living and integral part of my dream and it will take the pains of conception, carriage, and delivery to birth that dream and bring it to realistic proportions.

*"Many daughters have done virtuously, but THOU excellest them all"* **(Prov. 31:29).** To the Passion of my life, may the fire never die. Remain pure and undefiled.

**Your price is not negotiable.**

# INTRODUCTION

Beloved, We live in a world of insecurity. From weather to politics, science to human relationship, nothing seem to hold or work. Civilization, the god of 20th century man has neither assured us a secured future nor a safe passage. The frightened wife, the blank stare in the eyes of a hungry child, the intimidated teenage rebel who sees a meal ticket in his lethal weapon; the teenage prostitute who cannot understand or handle the emptiness within, are all realities we must grapple with and tame.

Fear and phobia like a two-some terrorist has held mankind hostage since creation. Abuse has become synonymous with right. So rampant is its sting that our generation has been subjected to a caricature of the divine purpose for creation. In the carnage ravaging the land, one specie stands out, bruised and hurt, tender and fragile: **the Woman**. From infancy to childhood, from adolescence to adulthood, cutting across strata, color, creed and ethnic divide, the female gender has suffered emotional, physical and sexual abuse from the male community. From War zones to commercial interchange the story is one locus of shame for her essence has been negotiated. Ironically, her frustration has been in the area of her greatest need for fulfillment (according to design) and from the very one assigned to provide that fulfillment: **the Man.** Recoiling in confusion, fear and insecurity, this has lead to the clamor for rights and protection for women everywhere across the globe. Their near-death life has pushed them to form alliances for jaded survival instincts, a sign of the man's failure to provide a shield for the woman.

A voice has echoed and reverberated through the ages down to our time, the voice of fallen man in his fallen state,

*"The woman whom thou gavest to be with me, she gave me of the tree, and I did eat".*

**(Gen. 3:12).**

This insinuation and responsibility masking has kept the man perpetually subjected to frustration and bondage of satanic deception.

The deception cannot be farther than that. By failing to see the true source of his opposition and recognize his primary assignment, he has been sidetracked to a mortal disadvantage, engaged in a war of attrition.

In a world where man has created a niche for himself with a philosophy that is substandard and negates God's blueprint, the woman's definition in God's curriculum cannot be over emphasized. She is the reflector of God's mercy, compassion and love for man; the epitome of His beauty and completeness. The man's world cannot hold without her essence and presence.

This work is a reaction to the satanic negotiation on the lives of girls, daughters and the woman in general; the carnage, the depletion of divine substance and essence relevant to complement the man's role in fulfilling his God-given task of dominating and replenishing the earth.

The sexual abuse, the social dislocation and relegation, the mental disrobing of her honor and dignity beyond these, the spiritual negation and compromise on her destiny and eternal relevance.

In these pages, you will be taken through creation to catch a glimpse of the higher purpose from the divine perspective for what she was created and empowered to be. The deadly drama that occurred and the negotiation that began that was to tumble down the ages to our day.

Created and endowed with a price not negotiable, she has become the caricature of the divine portrait but through the blood, God's negotiable instrument in Jesus the Seed of the woman, she is fully restored.

Never again would she be looked at with disdain or treated as a thing: She is God's Word for man made flesh and relative to his need. Clear your mind, fasten your belt and navigate with me through God's course.

*"Woman, thou art loosed!"*
*Love,*
**EBI CHURCHILL SMITH**

# HER BODY: The Force of Relativity

*"In the beginning God created the heaven and the earth. And God said, let us make man in our image, after our likeness: and let them have dominion over the fish of the sea, and over the fowl of the air, and over the cattle, and over all the earth, and over every creeping thing that creepeth upon the earth.*
*And the LORD GOD formed man of the dust of the ground, and breathed into his nostrils the breath of life; and man became a living soul.*
*And the LORD GOD said, it is not good that the man should be alone; I will make him a helpmeet for him.*
*And out of the ground the LORD GOD formed every beast of the field, and every fowl of the air, and brought them unto Adam to see what he would call them: and whatsoever Adam called every living creature, that was the name thereof. And Adam gave names to all cattle, and to the fowl of the air, and to every beast of the field; but for Adam there was not found helpmeet for him. And the LORD GOD caused a deep sleep to fall upon Adam, and he slept: and he took one of his ribs, and closed up the flesh instead thereof; And the rib, which the LORD GOD had taken from man, made he a woman, and brought her unto the man.*
*And Adam said, this is now bone of my bones, and flesh of my flesh: she shall be called woman, because she was taken out of man;*
'*Even every one that is called by my name: for I have created him for my glory, I have formed him; yea, I have made him."*
***GENESIS 1:1,26; 2:7,18-23; ISAIAH 43:7***

"**GOD**"…that three-letter name brings a pause to all of creation. Silence reigns supreme and a deafening silence at that while adrenaline runs high and goose pimples bathe the skin. The working of nature and the universal order screeches to a halt and creation recedes to the background of insignificance. All is silent. All is dark. All is lifeless.

"**In**", steps God with grandeur and quintessential majesty bringing meaning, giving form and a definition to all that matters in mortality-**beginning**. He set the stage, paved the entrance and designed the platform on which to present a grand purpose: **creation**.

All the exegesis of Omniscience cannot unravel Him who is from everlasting to everlasting; *He who makes darkness His pavilion and rides upon the wings of the wind;* whose splendor the language of man cannot define. Our vocabulary would not suffice to accord Him due adoration. We stand helpless with words when we come to worship Him. The immortal one who inhabits eternity was preparing a stage where He could bring the mystery of infinity to manageable proportions. In the creation of the heavens and the earth God was making known, in a condensed form, *His eternal power and Godhead being understood by the things that are made* (**Roman 1:20**). The heavens comprising the planets, stars, the sun and moon with an asbestos of cloud formation covering the expanse of space above; the earth with its teeming population of creatures bubbling and thrusting with life, an ecosystem of biodiversity communicating in countless ways, giving their version of praise and gratitude to their Creator and Sustainer. The planets and constellation of stars in galaxy up high, the sun and moon riveted to their socket in orbit, all summing up our awesome milky way and revolving around the Center of all centers-**the throne of the most High God!**

The blend of creation in the heavens and the earth which makes up the natural world can be seen in many ways, as a cathedral built with God's own hands (Hebrews 3:4). Entering that sanctuary on a warm spring morning, we can sense that all of nature joins with us in worship of the Creator. *Earth and heaven reflect His rays, stars and angels singing their praise. Peals of thunder, field and forest, flashing sea and flowing fountain. All His works surrounding Him; Center of unbroken praise.*

As the ages roll on, the heavenly bodies are ever in motion, the moon revolving round the earth, the earth with other planets revolving round the sun, the sun with all the other solar systems joined by countless other creations, all unknown to man, revolving in awful grandeur around the Center of all centers: **the throne of the Almighty!**

It took five days of divine effort to erect this cathedral of creation. However, grand as it appeared, this sanctuary of praise was not complete without the voice of a rare species to crown the harmony. Walking down the aisle of that sanctuary to the sixth row of days, God introduced a unique clause. *"And God said, let us make man in our image, after our likeness: and let them have dominion… upon the earth."* A consensus of the triune and true God was reached to make man and this, in the image and likeness of God Himself.

The purpose: to have dominion, authority and supremacy over all things in the earthly realm. Being in His likeness was to make man serve a unique purpose: to subject and lead all of creation back to the Creator in service to His eternal order. Man was to act as a great pulpiteer in this sanctuary in leading creation's praise to the Maker of all things. Another dimension was that man would be the only creature with the capacity to worship; for worship must be in spirit and in truth **(John 4:23,24; Philippians 3:3).** Man was the only creature embodied with soul and spirit for God, the Creator, is Spirit.

It was not enough to have His image; he must also be imbued with His likeness to cultivate administrative prowess and perfection upon the earth.

The concept of creation had been in the Omniscient mind of God and in His grand setting, He was delivering that dream on the platter of time defined as **"beginning"**.

God's eternal purpose was being brought to fleshly proportions and perfection must prevail over precision to make His glory known. Man, His ambassador, would hold sway and promote divine interest in this realm of the material world.

Formed from the basic organic component of the earth generally called dust, this divine masterpiece had a different pattern from all other species of the dust configuration. He was patterned after the image or form of the Creator Himself and empowered by His breath, giving him a spirit and soul capacity to relate with God in worship and adoration.

Man stepped into creation's cathedral with a similitude of majesty that characterized God's grand entrance into time in **Genesis 1:1** which marked the beginning, for he carried His likeness being made in His image.

With the making of man accomplished and the definition of his assignment charged him, God stepped back to His eternal track. He who is from everlasting to everlasting does not slumber nor sleep (Psalm 121:4). The connotation of 'rest' given in **Genesis 2:2** refers to this stepping out of earthly routine and subjection to the 24 hour-day time frame that characterized the prior six days of creation. God's day is eternal and a thousand years in earthly terms can be a day from the eternal dimension and vice versa. He inhabits eternity and from Him definitions emerge. However, **'rest'** here is symbolic and relative for through it we can step out of the limitation and labor of time and have a feel of God's rest as revealed in Hebrews 4: 11.

The stepping in of **Genesis 1:1** was complemented by the stepping out of His majesty in **Genesis 2:2.**

Divine rest included the efficient execution and management of His will in all of creation. This, Adam the first began to administer in the earth as he called an earth conference of biodiversity, accorded names to each, defining their habitat and other intricacies of their existence. The aquaculture was not spared in this mental prowess of nomenclature. The finny tribe of the marine world in their diversity were covered and all named by Adam. Adam's definition of terms became God's approval. Unearthly mental clarity filled him up with joy and he longed for more. Next was the wonder of creation that lay at his feet. The blend of the ecosystem and climate in nature, the rising of the sun in itself was a divine glory proclaiming the truth, the simplicity, and the might of the Maker. The configuration of weather spinning summer warmth and winter cold he understood was to refresh his health and temper his environment. The black sky of the night, the starry vault dotted with trinkets of stars, was for his amusement as he goes to sleep, rest assured that God has a surprise-full day when he awakes. He could gaze and see above, the constellation of stars, the planets in galaxy and in all appreciate the beauty of the cosmos from a spot; an attribute of perfection displayed in vision and in understanding. We see this same attribute of perfection in Jesus, the second Adam, as He observed the mystery of nature and knew the numbers of hairs on our head **(Matthew 6:25-30, 10:29,30, 1Corinth. 15:45-47).**

Bringing his gaze downward, he beheld the majestic mountains and hills, the flashing seas and flowing fountains, the green fields and forests. The variety of creatures that dotted the landscape of the Garden; the richness and blend of colors, the instinct that propel them, making them act in their God given capacity and belch their praise to God, was fun to watch. Taking a walk along the ocean banks and watching the teeming life of the marine world that existed below the surface, he could view them perfectly and were all within his perspective. Above all, the variety of nourishment and food at his disposal, taking a bite of food and enjoying the thrill, he understood food to be God's love made edible. He took a cue from all he saw in creation and understood that God was communicating, in countless ways, the exceeding riches of His love and great heart to him. Everything-the small, the mighty, the insignificant-was designed to project that love. Purpose would only be achieved when man, on this side of the great divide, understands the communication and returns pure worship back to his maker. Communication became the fulcrum of the eternal triangle. Communication is one of the greatest wonders we find in creation. The communication skill of the Almighty is intricately awesome. Communication, the name of the puzzle, is a word we poorly understand but often use and in a bid to express ourselves, we end up extending the divide between us. Even the creatures of our world now have to be tamed for us to communicate with them. This, obviously, is a result of the fall. Creation spoke in audible tones interpreted only by Omniscient wisdom (Psalms 19:12). The ever-changing beauty of the heavenly scene, the sun's transforming rays on the sea and land, the color and cloud formations. The moon and stars, to consider the distance of these heavenly bodies, clumps of galaxies so vast in number and expanse that even broad human categories like light years become almost meaningless. Smallness gets even smaller and bigness gets ever bigger. The attempt to resolve the mystery by reducing it to manageable proportions becomes tempting. Adam beheld the complex creation and was hearing God speak, in audible tones, the beauty of His purpose. In the lion, God speaks of His strength and boldness; in the elephant, of His might and greatness. In the ant, of His wisdom; in the eagle, of His majesty and dexterity; in the snail of His assurance He will surely prevail for He is on the job, that though He may tarry He will surely prevail. In the chameleon of His power to enter man's circumstances and impact a change, giving color to his world. In the mountains of His everlasting steadfastness, through food, of His love and concern for nourishment for the total man. This and through countless other creation too wonderful for man, He speaks in whispers and in tones. With eyes fastened on this grand scenery, the mind generated unearthly worship too deep for voice to utter. It was a spirit-to-spirit communication with the Almighty. And in the cool of the day, God came down to commune with man in fellowship.

Rising up on a bright morning in the Garden, and beholding the earth shrouded by steamy halo of fog, he looked forward to another day of new discoveries with anticipation. Slowly, methodically and dependably, God's world moved on through its appointed cycles whether anyone was watching or not. The animals played and related being driven by an instinct put in them by the Creator. The fishes swam downstream and upstream compelled by a force beyond them. The birds flew, and landed and piped music, giving praise to God in tones justified only by Omniscient ears. The flowers grew because a force beyond them compelled them. The sun, with a splendor unparalleled spreading sheets of warmth and worship over earth's landscape; bathing, distilling and generating life to all and sundry. Fulfilling the command of the Creator. Returning back to base in the Garden, Adam discovered another dimension in the creation. He noticed the bond of companionship between creatures on the land, in the sea and the air, aside the blend of harmony that existed among them. Even the capacity to reproduce after its kind was found in each plant species. He watched as animals and birds paired up in their different habitat propelled by instinct, a force beyond them, male and female.

Certainly he watched them copulate. Feeling a surge of energy rise within him and looking around, he discovered he was alone and truly lonely.

Passion, different from the one of worship and work, was craving for definition and expression within him. It was passion that existed in a different form and found in the creatures all around him. Deep down in his soul, he noticed the void and discovered the need; the quest for a companion and in companionship with him.

God is not a God of after-thought like us. It is apparent that He was there all along, watching, waiting. The Omniscience of God entails that He knows the end from the beginning in all things regarding all matter in all time and eternity. He had a wonderful agenda to unfold and He, in His loving wisdom wanted man to be fully aware of it even without divine briefing. He wanted man to step up His mental frequency and log onto His mind to conceive this mystery, by observing the creation and understanding the concept of companionship that was revealed in the making of male and female of every creature. It was to be a **Mental Frequency Modulation (M.F.M).** Though made perfect and given all the attributes of perfection, God was stepping up Adam's mental capacity to divine frequency as he took stock of the creation and observed the equilibrium of purpose and design. He had fared well so far until this point when he struck the broadband of divine frequency. It is noteworthy to discover here that Adam did not ask God for a companion or wife, he need not for he now saw what God sees: **the need**. And once divine perspective was attained, the stage was set to meet that need. God rarely reveals to man anything he can find out for himself. It may prolong but in seeking he would find. This holds a major truth for us as believers and this is where the force of relativity comes, the reason for this chapter and the point where life unravels. This is the starting point of all God will do in our lives. Until you see what God sees, you never can relate with God's plan for your life or world and implement it forcefully. Adam had carried that force, that passion, since the day he was made but he never recognized the need in him or the purpose of the internal rumblings of passion yearning for expression within. This grew in him daily until he saw and understood what God had already spelt out through the message of creation, ***being understood by the things that are made*** **(Romans 1:20).** That he was made for connection; he was designed for companionship. Immediately this truth became unveiled as he beheld creation his eyes opened and his mind stepped-up to attain divine perspective of order and design, no force on earth was potent enough to stop him or God from meeting that need. The scriptures affirm:

> ***"And from the days of John the Baptist until now the kingdom of heaven suffereth violence, and the violent take it by force.***
>
> **(Matt.11: 12)**

The kingdom of heaven represents God's throne and administrative headquarters from where all of creation takes its cue and command. This is where the definition and destiny of mankind emits. Creation has been established to point us to the one-and-only God who has our benefit in mind and longing to help us discover purpose. Not until we attain focus by tuning our minds to His word, we cannot amount to much in life. Once the divine perspective is attained, we will impact upon our lives the plan and purposes of the creator with such force the Bible calls it **"violent"** (unstoppable). This can also be seen as the law of recognition, which leads to discovery and recovery.

The purpose and relativity of the woman could not be stopped, not even by the deceit of the serpent. She is a product of divine conception, carriage and delivery and therefore, not subject to frustration or negotiation of satanic plot. Upon discovery, God acted on Adam to meet that need.

> ***"And the LORD GOD caused a deep sleep to fall upon Adam..."***

Again sleep here is symbolic though literal. In essence, God was telling Adam that He had no part in the work though his' was the need, He, Jehovah, would meet that need without man's effort. ***For thine is the kingdom, and the power and the glory, forever.*** He had to shut down all the faculties of soul and spirit to meet that need so that man would fear before Him and to Him alone will recede the glory and praise. Our worthy Creator and Maker! This divine concept of the woman was a mystery and at that, Adam's mind had to connect to the mind of God to ratify that mystery. Mystery erodes our sense of competence so we struggle to explain it, to rationalize it. How God longs for us to come into the sanctuary, the inner court of creations' cathedral, to worship Him for whom He is. There are purposes too deep for us to understand: complex, compound and contradicting circumstances that does not fit any pattern of logic or symmetry. Forever groping in the dark, we tend to put the pieces together and analyze the puzzle but in all, we fall far short, not having the divine perspective nor understanding the purpose of it all.

A glimpse into His glory will end our confusion. The cure for this frustration is to receive the higher purpose of His divine calling, which is love. That even when the pieces of the puzzle does not fit and explanations are not given, as we worship and love Him unconditionally we will attain divine perspective and rejoice in divine wisdom!

In the comatose of deep slumber, God performed an all time operation of caesarian section to bring Eve out of Adam. The case this time was not from his womb but from the cradle of his affection: **the heart**. The dexterity of God was once again put to work and out came a creature. Rare, and with a touch different from other creatures, this one carried an essence and presence which gave her a price and that price was not negotiable. The divine purpose attached to her creation made her even unique, she was made specifically for the man. The force of relativity to the man was in the making of her body, the specifics. Omnipotent skill fashioned the body of the feminine gender. The face, like the morning sun ever radiant; the hair, like a crown of gold gracely placed; the breast, like a fountain that never runs dry; the hands, empowered with a touch that could soothe tensed muscles; the legs, like stately trees carrying a bouquet of flowers and fruits above; the voice, that speaks of the goodness of God to bring assurance to man's soul; the eyes, speaking inaudible tones of the love and compassion of God the Maker; the heart, fashioned to accommodate man unconditionally, and joining countless other details of soul and mind to form a body complete and real. These were blended into a physique, giving it a finishing that could tantalize the most hardened of the male species, breaking him, flexing the rigidity of mind and muscle and causing resurrection and refreshing to the weakness of men. Brought before him, perfect Adam immediately went into mental geometry propelled by this physical vision and he could not be far from infallibility when he coined her **"woman"**, being bone of his bones and flesh of his flesh. He needed no divine briefing, he came from God and he carried the seed of perfection, an atom of the divine mind. Man's flawless capacity to give names was generated by vision, what he sees **(Gen. 2: 19).** This is an integral part of every man, the capacity to see, identify and relate with, is God's special design for the man. The phrase *"and God saw that it was good"* appears seven times in the story of creation recorded in Genesis 1, after which God certified creation *"very good"* at the end **(Genesis 1:4, 10,12,18,21,25,31)**. Man couldn't do otherwise when he first saw Eve the woman. He was able to encapsulate God's mercy and compassion for him into a five-star word 'W-O-M-A-N' and God was pleased at this first introduction and union. God's purpose was complete and fulfilled as mentally empowered Adam called this creature the very name He purposed, which was a key to her function.

    She became a blend of purpose and design; a divine masterpiece .She was God's poem to Adam. The divine Poet was, in essence, saying to man, *"you are caught up in a world of deep mysteries with ever expanding discoveries on the horizon but don't try to analyze it, to manage it. You must enter into the mysteries and celebrate them; rejoice in it, respond to it with poetic rhythm and praise. Trust me even when you cannot track me. My ways are past finding out!"* The body of the woman became the force of relativity God would use to communicate this dimension of truth to the man.

God is delighted in our poetry. For in appreciating that body would generate the product of passion in man- inspiration and worship. Latent force, volcanic, surging up in his soul likes molten lava and spilling over in strangely moving language. Man was basically designed for worship of his creator and it was not yet obvious how deep and profound this could be. In uniting with that body and feeling the depth of refreshing in his soul, he would have a foretaste of the deeper spiritual intimacy he could have in spirit and truth with God. Passion would produce the relative force. Poetry is the product of passion. God's purpose was to have man worship Him with unconditional love, so He composed a poem, wrapped it up in the body of the woman and gave it to man. He knew man would have to maintain focus on the objective, ward off distractions and ultimately create a dream-friendly environment. Man had begun to dream. The making of the woman was God's answer to man's quest, in fleshly proportions. She was designed and empowered to protect that focus, reduce distractions and complement that climate where the man could birth his dreams and watch them grow.

In fulfillment, passion of worship would then emerge and flow from their hearts. Adam was made originally from the dust of the earth and synonymous with dirt but Eve came out of Adam. This was another configuration of God's poem in the making of the woman. She was in a sense 'refined dust' and that body was designed to complement the physical make of the man; like the recycling process where new things are made from already existing material. In this correlation, Eve became a recycled form of Adam made from the raw material of Adamic tissue, however, without breaking down the existing material completely. In this way, Adam will appreciate the refined flesh in the form of Eve given him, and Eve would be attracted to the crude form of her man Adam. The fusion of these bodies will create a perfect complement and produce a blend of purpose by design: **the crude complementing the refined.** The ensuing force of relativity would introduce man to another dimension of worship to his Creator.

On the other hand, whenever the pressure of work assails and the tension of passion calls, he could reach to that body for affirmation, rest assured that God has all his need covered. She acted in this capacity as a circuit -breaker and a pressure valve to the man. God's immaterial (spiritual) word that brought the universe into existence had to be made flesh, tangible and material in form, for it to have the force of relativity to man in no other way represented in the creation

**(John 1: 4).** The woman's body became the answer. Though created and made equal in spirit i.e. in the image of God, it was the body function God spelt out in purpose by design in the making of that body. Man had tasted food and understood it to be God's love made edible. He had to taste something better to understand another dimension of God's essence and purity, in a relative way. The beauty of all, the tender mercies and the compassion of God were revealed through that body. The woman was made to reflect these eternal virtues of the Omnipotent God. Her purpose came from God and her presence was intended to provide man with God's assurance and to protect his focus on God's assignment for his life. This gave her eternal relevance, her worth and a price not negotiable. So long as she maintained the divine endowment of her price and relevance by sticking to her man, the man was destined to fulfill his mission. Any negotiation on her price would change the order, God's arrangement, and ultimately affect the man. *"For Adam was first formed, then Eve"* **(1 Timothy 2:13).**

Woman empowerment does not come by clamor for rights or recognition. She has been created and endowed with divine essence and presence, which gives her a price and her price is not negotiable. It takes a man to pay that price fully. Any compromise or negotiation would violate her purpose and only in the maintaining of that price can she fulfill her purpose and become all she was created and empowered to be. Her role and relativity to the man cannot be over emphasized. With this socio-spiritual (mind and body) equilibrium maintained by the woman's essence and presence in the man's world in place, he could focus on the objective of earth's administration and dominion, his primary task, head on.

Man needed praise, one to cheer him on the job and accord him due regards. He needed assurance and food, beyond the edible, soul provender. Man needed support, a companion to stand by him and complement his function. Man needed a healer, when his ego is bruised and battered. One to revive his fighting spirit and remind him that he was born to conquer, to dominate, to subdue; that the earth is his parish and, like the eagle he was made for the heights, born for heavenly adventures. Man needed a reward, to see his conquest and prowess reproduced in his seed and occupying his conquered territory. Man needed an answer from God to contain the mystery of it all and the woman became God's answer. Fashioned in like passion, flesh and blood, she was the container of God's full answer and man couldn't miss it. Yet he missed it…

**"Now the serpent was more subtle than any beast of the field which the LORD God had made. And he said unto the woman, Yea, hath God said?" Gen 3:1.**

The breeze was warm and delicate, and sheets of laughing sunlight danced through the leafy umbrella. "Praise God for a beautiful day!" Eve must have mused to herself as she beheld the fruits on the stately but mysterious tree. Satan was however nearby, not praising God with her, lurking, having waited for this grand moment. Using the familiar craftiness of the serpent and exploiting the suspense generated by the tree, he engaged the woman in a dialog relating to God's purpose for their lives; how familiar a terrain. Satan uses our most sensitive issues to lead us astray and violate the very thing we are least aware: God's purpose for our lives. He knows if he can cause us to veer from divine direction for our lives, we would spend a lifetime groping in the dark and fighting a faceless enemy in a war of attrition. Being lord of darkness, he would then manipulate our lives to his advantage and propagate his interest in the earth, the perfection of this subterfuge will then rope in generations as yet unborn; creating a subtle deflection of purpose.

The devil was negotiating God's price on the woman when he ignored the man and beguiled the woman. He knew something about the woman, which the man never understood or carelessly ignored. He could not confront the man because his mind had attained focus, the divine perspective, the godly viewpoint of perfection and order, which made him forceful in implementing the divine commission.

The woman was, however, God's gift to the man, a need intended to protect his focus, reduce distractions and, create a climate of protection where he could brood his seed and propagate the earth, thereby fulfilling the divine mandate. This was her price, her essence and relevance, defined.

With his mind tuned to divine frequency, all Satan needed to cut off the transmission and break man's focus was to negotiate the woman's price and the negotiable instrument became the fruit (the quest for knowledge and clamor for right; little wonder this clamor still reverberate in the world today). The woman was meant to be a reminder to the man of God's assurance that he would not fail, and her body was the relativity needed for the propagation of his seed and the maintenance of his assignment. God had designed that the propagation of the human race should be done through the marriage union. This was God's method of propagating the human family in a pure way to ensure and maintain purity, a divine essence necessary for His presence in creation.

She reached for the fruit of the tree after careful examination, mentally tantalized and visually captivated, took a bite and gave it to her husband "with" her.

In a moment, the workings of nature and the universal order screeched to a halt at the unfolding of this diabolic drama. All was silent; all became still and all trembled at the act of man, their ruler and king, upon transgressing the command of God, their Maker and Sustainer.

The celestial membrane of purity and perfection that permeated creation had been punctured and in seeped sin, an alien dark and diabolic, with a sickle of death in one hand and the scale of justice in another; personified and embodied in Satan. In a flash their eyes were opened (satanic awareness) and they saw that they were naked. Naked, stripped of the covering of God's glory. With sin came the depletion of divine substance and essence in the woman and the destruction of God's capacity and armor of authority in the man **(Roman 3:23)**. This was only the beginning.

Creation waited for the divine verdict as nature receded to the background trembling **(Roman 8:19-22, Habakkuk 3:3-11, Psalm**

**76:7-8).** Having succeeded, Satan could now negate the woman's price, her empowerment and function in protecting the man's focus, and interrupt his assignment thereby thwarting God's purpose. Satan's premeditated infiltration worked out vertically, to cut off man from his God and horizontally, from his assignment. All he needed to perfect the decay was to violate that body and destroy the relativity. The fruit of the tree of the knowledge of good and evil became the negotiable instrument, which ultimately violated their bodies, destroyed their function and dissipated their purpose.

The negotiation was complete and finished **(Romans 3:23; 5:17-19, 1 Cor. 15:21,22).** The man was there "with her" helpless, the divine frequency transmission blocked, his mind darkened, he became estranged from the God he could no longer understand or trust, **having believed a lie (Ephesians 4:18).**

"In" stepped God again to the track of time to seek for man but man was amiss and hiding from the Omnipresent One, an irony. Then God asked, *"Where are thou...?"* (Gen. 3:9). When the Omniscient God puts forth a question, He is obviously not seeking for information; He is seeking to help man discover himself and return to position. **(John 1:12, 11 Cor. 5:17, Rom. 6:23, 10:9,10,13; Eph. 1:7,2:1-5; Proverbs 28:13).** Man's response to God however, showed no remorse but was one of pride and rebellion.

> *"The woman whom thou gavest to be with me, she give me of the tree, and I did eat."*
>
> **GEN. 3:12**

He masked his responsibility by attributing his failure to the woman, God's priceless gift **(Pro. 31:10).** The deception could not be father than that. When a person begins to conclude that he or she is being disliked or hated by the Almighty, demoralization is not far behind. Satan will use their pain to make them feel victimized by God. What a diabolic trap! By failing to see the true source of his opposition and recognize his primary assignment, man was now sidetracked to a mortal disadvantage; engaged in a war of attrition.

Standing in the shadows, Satan's negotiation pact would be unleashed on humanity, chiefly introduced and propagated by the woman. With this achieved, every seed born would be deformed in mind, in purpose and ultimately, in relativity to God and the divine assignment. This will work to violate fulfillment, the purpose for creation.

Man became disqualified as a candidate for divine mercy, for it is written *'God resisteth the proud, but gives grace to the humble'* **(James 4:6)**. Again, *though the LORD be high, yet hath he respect unto the lowly: but the proud he knoweth afar off'* **(Psalm 138:6)**.

Divine verdict was pronounced following man's rebellion and the entire creation plummeted headlong into the abyss of the curse, groaning in travail **(Romans 8:19-22)**. God's perfect justice was meted to all parties.

> *"And the LORD God said unto the serpent, because thou hast done this, thou art cursed above all cattle, and above every beast of the field; upon thy belly shalt thou go, and dust shall thou eat all the days of thy life.*
>
> *And I will put enmity between thee and the woman, and between thy seed and her seed. It shall bruise thy head, and thou shalt braise his heel.*
>
> *Unto the woman he said, I will greatly multiply thy sorrow and thy conception; in sorrow thou shalt bring forth children; and thy desire shalt be to thy husband and he shall rule over thee.*
>
> *And unto Adam he said, because thou hast hearkened unto the voice of thy wife, and hast eaten of the tree, of which I commanded thee, saying, thou shalt not eat of it: cursed is the ground for thy sake; in sorrow shalt thou eat of it all the days of thy life;*
>
> *Thorns and thistles shall it bring forth to thee; and thou shalt eat of the herbs of the field; In the sweat of thy face shalt thou eat bread, till thou return unto the ground; for out of it wast thou taken: for dust thou art, and unto dust shalt thou return."*
>
> **GEN 3:14-19.**

The serpent was cursed above all the beast of the field and Satan, who embodied the serpent, was unmasked and dealt with. The divine verdict spelt his doom; **the seed of the woman would crush him.**

The Omniscience of God was displayed as the negotiation pact Satan thought would be in his favor was reversed by the prophetic decree.

A master at deception, Satan stood at the threshold of vast humanity to reap a grim harvest and perpetuate his diabolic agenda, in reversal to the divine purpose, on earth. This would be achieved primarily through the woman by branding a trademark of rebellion on every seed born, he would multiply his stock in humanity sparing no soul, so long as it comes through the avenue of birth. Adam, the first man, had received this venom of sin polluting his blood and life, which transfers naturally to his seed. God's pronouncement, however, challenged the satanic agenda and changed the tide to divine triumph. The seed of the woman (specific) would crush the head (negotiation pact) of Satan and break the yoke over mankind. The fulfillment of this prophecy came through Jesus Christ, our Lord, who was born not of the seed of man but through a miraculous infusion in the womb of a 'virgin'. The virginity of Mary was strategic as the purity of that body was relative to God's purpose and the blood of Jesus (the seed of the woman) spilled on the cross became God's negotiable instrument in undoing the negotiation pact of Satan on humanity.

God worked alongside the legal bid of Satan to satisfy the demands of His perfect justice. It was a battle of negotiation and legal transactions; from Satan it was the fruit of the tree of the knowledge of good and evil to make man a false demigod; from God it was the blood of Jesus Christ, His Son, the seed of the woman; *who was delivered for our offenses, and was raised for our justification* **(Romans 4:25).** *In whom we have redemption through his blood the forgiveness of our sins, according to the riches of his grace* **(Eph.1: 7).** *Unto him that loved us, and washed us from our sins in his own blood, and hath made us kings and priests unto God and his father; to him be glory and dominion forever and ever. Amen.* **(Rev 1:5,6).**

The negotiating table in this drama became mankind for he was made with a sovereign will, a power of choice independent of manipulation. God holds man responsible for his moral choices. If he chooses God he would be saved and restored to divine position, which was his original creation. If he reaches for the fruit of the tree of the knowledge of good and evil (rebellion), he would be infested with the sin virus and become satanic-in-nature. On the cross Christ was made SIN **(Satanic-in-nature**, specified) for us, though He knew no sin, that we might be made the righteousness of God in him **(11 Corinth 5:21),** for He embodies and personifies God's perfect righteousness.

Significantly noted, the job description and primary function of Adam and Eve, his wife, were spelt out by God, coming at a time when purpose had been violated in disobedience to God's law; for sin is the transgression of the law of God **(1 John 3:4).**

The first divine verdict pronounced bordered on the essence and price of the woman. Her purpose had been negated even before she conceived. The multiplier effect of this would mean Satan holding sway over the race of Adam, quoting a share on every seed born by the woman. Registering a trademark of rebellion, multiplying satanic interest and propagating his diabolic agenda throughout the world.

For this, God's first arrow of reprisal struck Eve, the medium of Adamic propagation, affecting her function, multiplying the process (length) and procedure of childbearing in **SORROW**.

Apparently, childbearing was meant to be a pleasurable and joyful anticipation, even the length of conception was prolonged as revealed in God's judgment. Alas, anxiety and fear now prevail over the pregnant of women. In essence, God was saying to the woman, *"You have ignorantly bargained your worth with Satan, my arch enemy, and given him a right to every seed to be born. Consequently, I will put friction in the system of propagation that you may know the pain in my heart; for my dream of multiplying myself in Adam and his seed you have foiled. Be gone!"*

Caught in the middle between God and man she realized, perhaps for the first time, the force of her relativity and the mortal reversal and friction in God's agenda caused by her transgression. Nevertheless, the Omniscient God in His mercy prophesied a restoration to purpose and perfection, to come through a unique seed of the woman.

Christ indeed was bruised (in His death) but He crushed the head of the serpent, breaking the negotiation pact of Satan forever, to redeem man. Adam ultimately was God's dream of propagating Himself, His glory and power, in fleshly proportions. And the woman's relative function made her the chief tool for this extension programme. Her primary function was to nourish the man, which was necessary to streamline him to excellence and productivity in the earthly realm well before he brings forth his seed to share in the enterprise of dominion. This divine purpose infused into the man's function we see outlined in scripture even before Eve came to the scene (Gen 2:15,19,20). The curse dealt directly with this function.

At the fall, a spiritual **'black hole'** occurred and purpose could no longer radiate. The loss of purpose permeated the realm of the material creation and nature began to work in reverse due to the fog of spiritual darkness resulting from man's transgression.

The earth, which was originally surrounded by a canopy of moisture that produced a subtropical, greenhouse-like condition in the climate and weather, filtering the radiation of the sun to suit life, became cursed by the sentence of God, the same word of authority that created it. During the flood, the very first but torrential rain, a direct result of God's large-scale judgment on rebellious man, that canopy collapsed, wreaking havoc with the world's climate, forever to change things.

Originally made a reflector of divine splendor, sin caused a deflection in the woman. Like Lucifer, her body (God's relative force to the man) was corrupted as it turned man's attention to itself **(Isaiah 14:12-19 Ezek. 28:11-19).** Just as God created the stars to shine and radiate light, some eventually turn the light back to itself and thereby 'pass out; forming **a black hole and the graveyard of stars.** In the debacle, Eve sort of 'passed out' as she turned God's light and relativity in the creation of her body back to herself. The purity of her body was strategic if the race of Adam would be propagated in a pure way. Sin had found a home in that body accompanied by

God's curse. From this disadvantage, the divine charge given in **Gen. 1:28** to replenish the earth and multiply would now work in reverse: ***"deplete the earth… relegate dominion, loose control…pollute the habitat; the land, sea, the air… (Yet) multiply.***

This pollution, beyond the land, sea, and air of the environment, we now see in our bodies, in our health and social practices reaching frightening and pandemic proportions. And of these the woman is most affected. It is noteworthy to mention here that the fulfillment of prophecy regarding her salvation and the breaking of the negotiation pact was connected to her child bearing and faith (in God's forgiveness through the blood) **(1 Timothy 2:14,15)**. This is a direct and true revelation of the purpose for her body: **to propagate the seed and increase God's awareness in mankind.**

The close of this book will deal with God's reaction to the satanic negotiation and how it worked to restore the woman in relativity to God's purpose and the man's effectiveness. The virtues and relativity of the woman cannot be over emphasized. Meanwhile, long before the fall something beautiful was portrayed upon creation of the woman. A beauty which filled man with suspense…. **she was naked!**

# HER NAKEDNESS: The Beauty of Suspense

*"And they were both naked, the man and his wife, and they were not ashamed.*

*And the eyes of them both were opened, and they knew that they were naked, and they sewed fig leaves together, and made themselves aprons.*

*Unto Adam also and to his wife did the LORD GOD make coats of skins, and clothed them.*

*Now when I passed by thee, and looked upon thee, behold, thy time was the time of love; and I spread my skirt over thee, and covered thy nakedness: yea, I sware unto thee, and entered into a covenant with thee, saith the Lord GOD, and thou becamest mine.*

**GENESIS 2:25; 3:7; 21; EZEK. 16:8.**

*'And they were both naked, the man and his wife, and they were not ashamed!*

The connotation and emphasis on nakedness in this single verse of scripture cannot be overlooked. It highlights a unique design, which portrayed a beautiful truth. This was long before the fall. God's design left no detail out in the making of the woman.

All she was, in essence and relativity, pointed to the man and was for the man's pleasure and fulfillment. Her presence and the essence endowed on her was to serve to reduce distractions, thereby maintaining the man's focus and streamlining him to excellence in his primary assignment. It is apparent that God had the man's pleasure paramount in mind as seen in the light of scriptures. His assignment of dominating the earth was in the path of least resistance from his subjects. He was to oversee creation in the administration and execution of God's will on earth and God had put all things under his feet **(absolute authority psalm 8:3-8).** For man to have His likeness he must have a test of divine pleasure, albeit, in fleshly proportions.

Scriptures affirm that *in the presence of God there is fullness of joy, and at His right hand are pleasures forevermore.* Again, we are told that He created all things for His pleasure, as they are and were created **(Psalm 16:11; 36:5-9 147: 10, 11; Revelation 4:11.)** What this implies is that the efficient working of all things created, according to design and purpose, was to generate pleasure and joy in the presence of the living God and Maker of all things.

Even when the creatures were not informed of the purpose of their Maker, they were, nevertheless, compelled by a force beyond them to do His bidding, singing their praise to His glory **(Habakkuk 3:3; Psalm 19:1,2; 104: 24-32, 145: 10-12; 148: 1-4).** The clause here is that man, the crown of creation and fashioned in His likeness, does not need to be compelled to worship God. He would sit on the adjacent throne of authority on this side of the great divide and, with creation perfectly in view, appreciation will spring up in his heart, generating pure worship to his Maker. The beauty of this configuration is that he would come to terms in understanding the purpose of it all. This was the crown, the objective, and the purpose of God the Maker. The making of the woman's body clarified this grand purpose.

A poem I composed in anticipation for the girl of my dreams gives an insight into this setting. Titled "**Bed of Our Passion**", the third verse reads,

> *'On the bed of our passion we will lay*
> *God's orchestra producing harmony*
> *Only to those who follow the lead*
> *Of the great choirmaster of our lives*
> *A symphony composed by grand design*
> *Man and woman created and empowered*
> *Equipped with the seed and the womb.*

The making of the man and the woman can be seen as God's orchestra (a combination of different parts in design and in function) intended to produce harmony (as in music). However, this could only be achieved as they followed the lead of God, as the great Choirmaster of their lives. Their intricate design was in consonance with a symphony composed by God; as man and woman were created and empowered, equipped with the seed and the womb.

The aspect of creation designed to produce that pleasure in man was the nakedness of the woman. This nakedness satisfied the mental suspense in the man and aided in his imaginative creativity.

As highlighted in chapter one, man is a mentally charged creature. His mental frequency is charged by what he sees. When he saw perfection and purity enveloping the realm of creation, his mind generated praise and worship to God. He enjoyed every bit of what he saw and upon this, he was inspired to give names to all creatures. In perfect infallibility, he named them all according to design and function without divine briefing.

Earlier, God, in the creation, **"saw"** all that He had made and pronounced them *'very good'* **(Genesis 1:31).** His pleasure is derived from the fact that *all things are naked and opened unto the eyes of Him with whom we have to do; neither is there any creature that is not manifest in His sight.* Even the darkness of the night shines as the day, for both are alike before Him.

**(Hebrews 4:13; Psalm 139:1-12; Jer. 17:9-10).**

The everlasting arm bears the weight of His creation, you and I inclusive. The Omnipresent eye maintains equilibrium in the universe. The Omniscient mind understands every motive, knows every pain we bear and willing to share.

Above all, we have the Omnipotent assurance that He will never leave us nor forsake us. God, the eternal all sufficient all wise one, knows all things. And this is His glory and pleasure. A fraction of this infinity was revealed in fleshly proportion, portrayed by the woman's nakedness. This nakedness was both relative and absolute. She was placed before the man in bare nudity and every detail of that nakedness was for the pleasure of the man, bodily and mentally. Her absolute nakedness, however, was unveiled in sexual intercourse. In the likeness of God, man was made to behold that nakedness and receive mental gratification.

His mind was made perfect and that body would produce perfect pleasure understood only by the mind of a man. Beyond actual sex, he would achieve mental equilibrium as he related with God and his environment, which formed his work. The woman's nakedness and the intricacies of her body design satisfied perfectly the suspense in the mind of man. Man's ability to see and his field of vision increases his mental capacity and generates pleasure in him which tunes him to God in worship. Man was to satisfy his curiosity with that nakedness and, mentally charged, the pure pleasure derived would erupt gratitude and praise to the Creator. His creative imagination was propelled by that nakedness. Initially, man first imagined a companion for himself when he had none. He had taken stock of the creation and observed the concept of companionship displayed, upon this; he imagined or formed an image of a likely companion in his mind.

God then acted upon that mental image, which was in accordance with His perfect agenda, and made Eve, the woman **(Genesis 2:18-23).** God waited for man to step-up his mental capacity to His order, in creating that image mentally, before meeting the need. It therefore follows that whatever the mind of man can create, it can achieve. This also is in accord with God's likeness, for we are made in His likeness (character) and image (form) **(Genesis 6:5; 8:21; 11:6; Deut. 31:21; Proverbs 6:16,18).**

Imagination is the act of creating mental images of what has never actually been experienced. The power to imagine is God's special gift to man and it is an endless maze of power. Whatever the mind of man can imagine or create it can bring to pass.

Jesus, the second Adam, demonstrated the control that God originally intended us to have **(John 5:19).** The fact is that we **"see"** (imagine) things all the time and we **"see"** things before we do them, but only when our power to "see" gets united with God's power to **create** do we see miracles. And they happen because that is what God's originally intended. Adam was able to **"see"** (creatively imagine) Eve before God brought her to manifestation, his mind having logged on to God's mind to conceive the mystery. The woman's nakedness was both relative and symbolic, streamlining man's mind to the pure and perfect, which made it beautiful and ennobling in all-purpose and relevance.

In the drama of the debacle, the first awareness that struck the couple upon eating the forbidden fruit was that they were naked.

This was even before they grappled with the reality of their transgression of the divine command not to eat of the tree. Satanic awareness made them first see their nakedness and they become filled with shame even in the presence of each other (a shame indeed). The corrupted mind saw shame in nakedness. The spiritual nakedness became obvious as they fled from God's approaching presence and hid themselves. Satan knew something that the man ignored to his mortal dismay. He knew if he could violate that body he would thwart the purpose and break the relativity needed for the man to accomplish his mission, the divine mandate.

Furthermore, he schemed to deify the fallen body of the woman making it alluring to fallen man and fanning the embers of Eros within him, turning his focus from God, and thereby introducing darkness into the mind (creativity) of man by exploiting his power of suspense. Under darkness, this was achievable without man detecting or challenging him.

However, God was fully aware for in His Omniscience and loving wisdom, He made man and fitted him with a beautiful suspense that would make him seek after Him. And after the fall, he moved to provide man and woman with clothing of skin. Though a pseudo covering, as compared to His glory that covered them before the fall, it served to protect that suspense in man and the deflection that could occur in their fallen state. The woman being clothed could still serve the relativity of purpose and safeguard the beauty of suspense, undressing only when it becomes necessary for the man's nourishment and pleasure. However, this was not to be as it was apparent that Satan was waiting to have them in his full circle of negotiation where he would perfect the decay. They were cursed and driven from the garden, from God's love and perfection, from God's provision and protection. Cut off from fellowship; driven from God's paradise and out into a wild weird world, a world where darkness, more dense than fog, could suffocate the soul. A world ruled by fear and where your shadow becomes an intimidation.

A world where the sting of death, an alien, was certain and its shadow spread like a curtain, made the world a valley of depression. A world ruled by Satan, whose very nature and venom is infested in the blood of all mankind and transferred through childbirth, suppressing the challenge or resistance of man thereby. The decay spread like wildfire and this has tumbled down through generations to our day. Beginning with primordial man, the earth with a handful of people became corrupt beyond recall. With the emphasis on the violation of the woman's nakedness, the deflection of purpose could not be otherwise as early in the record of beginnings the sons of God "saw" the daughters of men and lusted after their bodies **(Genesis 6: 1-4).**

The result became the increased number of weird men abounding in their acts of wickedness. Significantly noted, this emanated from their depraved and deflected power of imagination fuelled by that nakedness. Every conceivable evil was actualised while disorder and anarchy prevailed upon the earth. A spiritual **'black hole'** had occurred and purpose could no longer radiate. This loss of purpose permeated the earth with darkness and caused creation to work in reverse, groping in the fog of spiritual darkness.

With the woman's nakedness violated, that deified body now turned the attention of man to itself, pulling down the very sons of God as victims early in Satan's negotiation harvest
**(Genesis 6:4,5; Peter 2:4,5; Jude 6).**

The corridors of history is strewn with the carcass of the vanquished of humanity owing to the violation and exploitation of the woman's nakedness which invariably leads to evil imagination and acts of men.

Kings and servants, princes and paupers alike, the mighty, the low and the revered, even the anointed of God (from the beginning) were not spared the bid of the negotiator of souls, the venom of sin; the satanic nature **(Judges 16; 11 Sam 11: 1-5; 1Kings 11:1-8; Neh. 13:26)**

Samson the anointed judge; David the king, a man after God's own heart; Solomon a man imbued with a rare combination of God's matchless wisdom and a poet of all time, to mention but a few. These and many more were affected by sin's seductive art. And are we any different in our time from those of antiquity?

We ought to cover our faces in shame and cry unto God for mercy as Satan, in his unflagging aggression, has perfected the art of deceit. With the battle set in array against the Church, God's medium of affecting society and impacting the world, we seem to be loosing ground.

Society is bombarded with the false deity embodied in the exposed flesh of the woman. Nakedness is everywhere, on the street, in the market, the work place, in the school (apology), everywhere outside the bedroom. Most shameful, it is now in the church of Jesus Christ, right on the pews as Satan is bent on stripping the last straw of clothes God used in covering Eve, the woman, and leave her naked in rebellion.

A generation of naked rebels is fast covering the land and the imminent societal earthquake will measure high on the Richter scale. A wasting generation; a hapless, helpless and hopeless existence people call life is right before us in full glare; the carnage, the depletion of divine substance in the woman, the failure of the man owing to deflection of purpose for living.

Right before our eyes the ladies, sisters and daughters of the evangelical race, are being swept in this tide. Kidnapped royalty, taken hostage by Satan and they are a key to the sustenance of the men, the boys and the sons of God.

God gave specific laws to keep His provision of cover permanently clad to our bodies especially relating to women **(Leviticus 18:1-19).**

In the New Testament, Jesus warned about looking on women to lust after them in the heart **(Matt. 5:28).** This goes primarily to the man and highlights man's power of imagination. This relates also to man's original sin when he first realized, of all, that he was naked.

Rebellion against God opened a new consciousness .**The illicit or unlawful unclothing of the body is still rebellion against God (Ezek 23:9-17; Ex. 32:25; Micah 1: 8-1).** The woman's nakedness has become a fascination today as Satan has perfected the art of holding man to suspense in rebellion.

Forever fascinated, tantalized, man reaches out for one more bite of the forbidden fruit. Fascinated by the gay glitter of naked flesh and with one detailed look at a nude woman, a man can generate all the materials needed to create a mental world of fantasy; an odyssey in fantasia. These immoral thoughts bring physical pleasure to the body. The sensations are pleasant and gratifying. The mind becomes programmed to renew this pleasure at the slightest provocation. In time, the mind needs no stimulus – it can create its own. Self-gratification becomes habitual and uncontrollable. Man sinks to perdition and pervasion which ultimately brings judgment of sin and death **(James 1:13 – 16; Roman1: 21-28; 8: 6-8; Eph 2:1-3; 4:17-19; Jude 8).**

Beyond the veil lies a beauty, God's design, that stupefies the senses and fills the imagination with creativity. That veil has been taken off in our generation and shredded and the stench of decay is fuelled through billboards, magazine stands, TV, movies, the Internet and blatant exposure on the streets and leisure reserves of our "advanced" world.

The world believes a lie because the news media have stepped way beyond their rightful place. They have an agenda and the resources to carry out that agenda. With their talent they have taken the foolish, the vile and the empty and make it awesomely appealing, while we, the redeemed of God, take unspeakable glory and a manifold cure and bungle our presentation as if we were lying. The world lies well and we tell the truth badly.

Consequently, the failure of the man in safeguarding the essence of the woman, and of his capacity in fulfilling divine purpose stinks to high heaven in our time. Hatred, divorce, wars and conflicts ravage our world, crimes of incredible propensity; these and many more has reached pandemic proportions today. The fall made man fail- God and himself.

The divine prophecy of the Seed of the woman has, however, turned the tide in our favour as Christ seeks to restore everyone from the curse, so many as put their trust in His saving power and all of whom trusting, they form members of His body, the church.

To the women, He wants to restore that body to honor and cover it with His glory and righteousness, giving it a veil of relativity and purpose again. To the men, He wants to restore focus and objectivity, the power of godly vision and imagination, necessary in fulfilling the purpose of creation. In all He encourages us as members of His body, the church, to renew our minds and heart for out of it proceeds the issues of life and to accept His righteous covering, lest we be found naked in rebellion **(2 Corinth. 5:3; Revelations 3:18).**

God wants you ladies to keep those veils down, covered in modesty and sobriety so you would appreciate the beauty of suspense for your man's gratification and mental empowerment. This will lead him to productivity and excellence, which he was created to achieve but consequential to your obedience to God's order.

In the original creation, the glory of God produced the perfect cover. The original creation is appreciated when the veil is taken away and she stands bare in the sight of the man. This, nevertheless, has to be God's approved mate for her in marriage; anyone outside that perimeter violates her purpose and dissipates the beauty of suspense generated by that nakedness.

With the right mate unveiling her nakedness for the first time, God has another dimension for bonding this masterpiece of relativity to her lover and fulfiller for life. Within that body was an entrance with pearly gates, leading to the subterranean chambers of a garden richer than Eden. **Her virginity: the priceless gift of bonding.**

# HER VIRGINITY: The Priceless Gift of Bonding

*"Therefore the Lord Himself shall give you a sign; Behold, a virgin shall conceive, and bear a son, and shall call his name Emmanuel.*
*And in the sixth month the angel Gabriel was sent from God unto a city of Galilee, named Nazareth.*
*To a virgin espoused to a man whose name was Joseph, of the house of David and the virgin's name was Mary. And she shall bring forth a son, and thou shalt call his name Jesus: for he shall save his people from sins. And (he) knew her not till she had brought forth her firstborn son: and he called his name JESUS.*
*And the word was made flesh, and dwelt among us, (and we beheld his glory, the glory as of the only begotten of the father,) full of grace and truth.*
*And of his fullness have all we received, and grace for grace"*
**(ISAIAH 7:14; LUKE 1:26,27; MATT. 1:21,25; JOHN 1:14,16).**

> *"So he drove out the man; and he placed at the east of the Garden of Eden cherubims, and a flaming sword which turned every way, to keep the way of the tree of life."*
>
> **(GEN.3: 24)**

The LORD God had driven man out of the garden and placed cherubic confronters (Angels) to keep the way of the tree of life. The fruit of that tree held the key to life everlasting as God affirmed **(3 vs.22)**; for this, God sealed access to the tree to stop fallen man from eating of it also and living forever. Man would look for another way to obtain eternal life.

Prior to this, Adam had bonded to Eve in the provision of her welfare and security. Through the manifold wisdom and love of God, the earth was created and put in place before the making of man. Man came to the scene and was given charge (dominion) over the earth; a perfect atmosphere of welfare and security. God made Adam know that he was in charge and that all creation was his subject. In this setting, Eve was made and brought before Adam. In due course, she came to understand that her man owned and ruled this paradise of beauty and order and in this, her welfare and security was assured. This was God's method of bonding the man to the woman, chiefly by making him capable of providing for her welfare and security.

However, God had another garden richer than Eden and more beautiful than the order displayed in the physical creation. A wellspring of life gushing from a fountain, deep in the subterranean chambers of a soul made like Adam. The entrance to this garden was marked with a special feature, a gate that upon entrance introduces man to another dimension of creation rather experienced than imagined. To the woman, it was a bonding of her mind and emotion, stronger than the affirmation of verbal covenant, to her man. A powerful soul merger occurred upon entrance to the garden. That garden became the body of the woman and its richness depicts sexual intimacy with man- the mystery being God's design of her virginity and the concept of bonding her to man through it. By this design, God was saying to the man, ***"you can have the woman to yourself for the rest of your life; in my creation which I have made*** *you a lord, I have empowered you with the capacity for providing her welfare and security which bonds you to her but that is not enough. I will also make her bond to you in her mind and emotion; she will cleave to you as long as she lives. For it is not the hole that makes the woman but the emotion that lubricates the hole. That emotion will bond her to you for the rest of her life."*

A man's ability to leave father and mother, depicting financial and economic independence, empowers and makes him cleave or bond to his wife **(Gen. 2:24)**. In the woman however, that cleaving or bonding will come through the first sexual union with the man she calls her husband.

*"And Adam knew Eve his wife; and she conceived, and bare Cain, and said, I have gotten a man from the LORD."*

**GEN.4: 1**

This verse is all embracing as it contains the first account of sexual intercourse, conception, carriage and delivery in one. And it happened within the perimeter of God's approval, **in marriage.** The result produced a child **FROM** God and Eve recognized this. Adam had been with his wife since she was created and given to him but sexual bonding brought a new awareness; he **"knew"** her. This knowledge was of one richer than the pleasures of Eden; a knowledge too profound for words to define but understood only by the soul of man that is nourished thereby.

The woman became bonded to the man in mind and emotion for life. Adam had bonded to Eve upon creation having provided for her welfare and security in the perfect environment of the garden. Eve was, however, getting bond through this first episode of sexual intimacy with Adam. The woman's price of bonding will be in the fulfillment of her most intense emotional experience and the shedding of blood in the breaking of her hymen through sex.

Biologically known as **"hymen"** (haimen), the hymen is a tissue of flesh that marks the opening of the reproductive cavity in a woman making a man's penetration impossible or difficult. A thin strand of flesh that distinguishes a woman with the virtue that makes her a "virgin"- one who has never been engaged in sex. It is the identity of the sexually undefiled among woman.

The emphasis is not on the presence or the absence of the hymen in a woman but on the state of her sexual purity, her virginity, before marriage. God designed it that Eve did not have a childhood or growing experience but made her a fully matured woman and brought her to Adam. She was to have firsthand the experience of every woman, of a strange but beautiful emotion, different from other experiences and the life-long bonding that goes into effect with her partner. Emotion, rather than feeling, was an integral part in the making of the woman. Emotion is a spiritual essence, an attribute of God, which was revealed chiefly in the making of the woman.

***"Like as a father pitieth his children, so the LORD pitieth them that fears him. The LORD is merciful and gracious..."*** (Psalm 103:13,8). This and in countless references abounding in scriptures God was letting us know of His compassionate reserve for man. He compares the emotion of pity, which bonded father and son, to His heart of mercy for the mass of humanity and creation at large.

Primordial man was yet to understand this divine concept of emotional bonding and its relativity to him. So God weaved the tissue of emotion into the fabric of the woman, making it her chief essence and the force of relativity to the man would come through sexual intercourse with her body, first introduced by the breaking of her virginity. This became the priceless gift of bonding the woman to man. This would make her cleave to the man as the chief fulfiller of her emotion thereby pouring out herself to him in nourishment and healing. Every other attribute or essence comprising her love, her virtue, beauty, passion and sexuality would be revealed through this channel of emotion. While emotion would rule her for life, God designed it that the bonding would take place in the first intercourse, which introduces that emotion. **He placed the hymen in her body, the breaking of which introduces that significant clause of bonding in her spirit.**

It was a spiritual connection that demanded physical confirmation- a physical act, which triggers a spiritual reaction of bonding. The woman's definition and relativity is connected to the man. Without man she is oblivious and fades into insignificance.

The larger story however, is God's purpose for this design and its relativity to the redemption story of mankind, which brought Jesus to earth. Due to the fact that sexual knowledge with a woman affects the man's mind (and world) in basic and fundamental ways, God put the hymen in the woman, which demanded confrontation and force to be broken, as a guard to the woman to ensure the worthiness of the intruder into her garden.

In like manner, the tree of life was guarded with cherubims and a flaming sword to ensure the worthiness of anyone desiring to eat of its fruit; for it contained the key to life eternal.

Only Jesus makes one worthy of the tree of life and Him alone can restore that which the intruder has destroyed when the woman is disvirgined outside wedlock. Although Satan had succeeded in making man sin in disobedience to God which perverted purpose and permeated the perfect atmosphere of the garden with a fog of fear and insecurity affecting all of creation.

Nevertheless, the act of God in safe guarding the tree of life was symbolic. It ensured that sin's permanence was not to be, as man could no longer eat of the tree of life, thereby reducing sin to mortality and death in the body of man. This made it possible for Christ's death in mortal flesh to redeem mortal man and break the power of sin and death in the body **(Romans 8:3; 1 Corinth. 15:19-26,44-56; Hebrews 2:14-16).**

Furthermore, it relates to the woman in the fact that if she keeps the gates to her life nourishing garden well guarded, even when other areas of the creation around her is been violated, she still can fulfill God's purpose in relativity to her making and for the man's fulfillment.

This became the precedent that brought about the virgin birth of Jesus through Mary. Mary had kept herself pure and the gate to her garden well secured which gave her credibility to relate God's purpose for the redemption of man through the supernatural virgin birth of the holy child Jesus. She was however, perfectly bonded to Joseph who later became her husband.

This truth was again portrayed in the Song of Solomon while king Solomon, under divine inspiration, offered a window of what the woman's sexuality was all about. In the last chapter of the song the woman recalls the conversation of her brothers when she was a child.

(S.O.S.8: 8,9).

*"We have a little sister, and she hath no breasts: what shall we do for our sister in the day when she shall be spoken for? If she be a wall, we will build upon her a palace of silver: and if she be a door, we will enclose her with boards of cedar."*

That she was little and had no breasts simply indicated that she was a child and not yet matured. In essence, the brothers protectively query, *"was our sister a wall?* Did she keep herself pure? Did she keep her garden gate secured, reserving herself for her faithful permanent lover? Or was she a door, violated by intruders and temporary lovers?

Grown up and matured, the woman firmly assured her husband with dignity,

*"I am a wall, and my breasts like towers: then was I in his eyes as one that found favor."*

**S.O.S 8:10**

She had not given into unbridled passion. Neither had she let in violators to her garden or allowed little foxes spoil the vines **(S.O.S.2: 15)**. The LORD give understanding to women and patience to the men, I pray! The wedding scene is graphically illustrated in **chapter 4**, where the man describes his bride-to-be as

*"A garden inclosed (locked) is my sister, my spouse; a spring shut up, a fountain sealed. A fountain of gardens, a well of living waters, and streams from Lebanon."*

**S.O.S 4:12,15.**

Then we come to the wedding night, the night of bonding her to the man of her dreams, when the woman calls out:

*"Awake, O north wind; and come, thou south; blow upon my garden that the spices thereof may flow out. Let my beloved come into his garden, and eat his pleasant fruits."*

**S.O.S 4:16.**

The clarity and relativity of these scriptures cannot be misunderstood. It reveals God's mind regarding His purpose by design of how man and woman should relate to reflect His glory in creation. The poetic landscape depicted in the above verses of scripture creates a picture in the mind, portraying the majesty of God.

Imagine a stage prepared for the union of two lives to be made one in marriage. The stage being nature's wild; the attendants, God and the Celestial hosts; the fragrance is the wind bringing God's approval and blessing. No other earthling is mentioned or present, just the couple. The landscape is bathed with translucent glory in a blend with nature's greenery. Gosh!

The grandeur, the breath taking scenery will erupt praise and generate worship from the deep recess of the soul. Fantasy? No, more real than the reality of this world which has become a cycle of monotony and frustration.

This, and much more than the mind could fathom, is God's design for man in flesh, and the woman is a strategic agent in fulfilling this glory on earth. For this, her price is not negotiable.

She should stake worlds and wealth to keep her pure sexually and fulfill purpose in bonding only to one man in the consummation of marriage, thereby bringing glory to God. Within the confines of that commitment, purpose will spring forth from permanence. Meditating along this line, I composed a poem (as highlighted in chapter 2) titled **"Bed of Passion."** The fourth verse reads:

*"On the bed of our passion we will deliver*
*Our dream our seed shall be conceived*
*To bruise the head of the serpent*
*Our heart shall be knitted as one*
*Our bodies locked in holy fragrance*
*The aroma of divine institution*
*A taste of paradise restored."*

This poem is a product of my creative thoughts for the girl of my dreams, which I spoke about before the introduction in this book. For her I have waited and kept my estate, praying for God's keeping power to uphold her as well. This was God's pattern before the fall, in bonding one woman to one man within the perimeter of permanence; and it remains God's pattern after the restoration through the blood, for God is the LORD who cannot change and in this we are assured. Premarital sex dissipates this purpose of bonding and corrupts the beauty of permanence. Only when man aligns his will to obey God and follow His moral purity imperative in obedience can he have the aroma of divine institution of marriage; a taste of paradise restored.

The heat is on in our generation as men, ruled by the satanic nature (**SIN**), are flagrantly violating God's purpose by design in the area of sexual bonding. Forcing even the gates and barriers to the reserved part of the garden meant for life bonding and nourishment. Some have gone so down the drain of deceit, hemmed in the vicious grip of the satanic negotiation cycle that they see all I am saying as old fashioned, an opium of religion. However, I am speaking from the arid region of the sexual divide where the heat is greatest and the temperature highest: **as a single**. The tropical reality can only be cooled in the oasis of God's purpose by design: **marriage.**

And it pays to wait for only in so doing can we follow the lead of God, the great **Choirmaster** of our lives and produce harmony as we bond to the right mate as man and woman created and empowered, equipped with the seed and the womb. *For he that shall come will come, and will not tarry* (Hebrews 10:37). Unfortunately, many women are married to men to whom they are not bonded. Their mind, will and emotion being bonded to someone else; somewhere, sometime the negotiation took place and they handed it over in premarital sex.

Having lost the price and relativity, her nakedness the beauty of suspense violated, her marriage becomes a union of bodies satisfying and fulfilling instinctive passion only. Downstream the soul remains divided in opinion and objective and two cannot agree as one.

Time sets in bringing wear and tear to that body. Her virginity, God's gift of bonding her to the man on the first night of married love being lost, her sexual life becomes frustrating and less satisfying as the law of diminishing returns takes over. Forever she is confused and depressed with the awesome *"why?"*

Her virginity was God's design to make her 'click' in the man for life.

"The blessing of the LORD, it maketh rich, and he addeth no sorrow with it." PROVERBS 10:22

The divine 'click' in her having been negotiated and sold out, she becomes like a cloud without water drifting in space, a fulcrum without support and a bow without arrow. Unable to relate the purpose of creation to the man in maintaining his focus, reduce his distractions, and complement the climate of protection where he can hatch his dreams and watch them grow; she becomes a source of his frustration and defeat.

Her purity is God's strongest weapon and website to launch a glorious destiny. It was the birth of Christ that broke the hymen of Virgin Mary not intercourse with Joseph. This was necessary to bring Christ as the second Adam without paternal link and free from the contamination of the sin virus in the Adamic blood. Nevertheless, Mary's marriage was still blessed and fulfilled as God, the sovereign and Omnipotent One, bonded her perfectly to Joseph.

Premarital sex introduces the satanic negotiator. When you comply with the satanic negotiator, you lose your price, your worth and essence, your relativity to your man (not men) and to God's plan and purpose for your creation. God cannot be mocked, for whatever you sow becomes your harvest now or future **(Galatians 6:7)**. The price of bonding was in the shedding of the blood in the breaking of the hymen. When that blood is shed premarital, outside the marital commitment to the welfare and security of the woman, her purpose is violated and her price negotiated. The blood creates a covenant and she, nevertheless, becomes bonded to a violator and negotiator thereby dissipating the purpose of relativity and the lifelong assurance of welfare and security God intended for her through the man approved of God as her mate.

To strip an unmarried woman of her virginity ensures that she will never be bonded to her true man, which violates God's word regarding the two becoming one. This lack of bonding will introduce division in the soul and ensure satanic interests springing in the home. Furthermore, every seed born in that home carries a trademark or seal of that negotiation pact in the woman, capable of reproducing the violation in their seed.

Violating the woman's virginity outside marriage meant breaking the Tamper-Proof seal and adulterating the content. A pseudo cultural mentality that despises the moral purity imperative of God takes root. The internal wound is mortal. The reverse of divine purpose goes into gear, decay sets in and the spirit begins to wither. Satan uses the media hype to market the lie of superficial upgrading that you can catch the fun and avoid the fire, but the word of God is explicit in **PROVERBS 6:25-28.**

The essence of women who marry as virgins ensures the delivery of seeds empowered to perpetuate the bruising of the serpent's head, the fulfillment of which took place at Calvary. For this, Satan, the negotiator, applies every art of seduction to destroy the virginity of women before marriage by negotiating sex.

There was no record of any sexual activity between man and wife prior to **GENESIS 4:1.** The Bible gives only details relevant to our understanding of God's character and His dealings with man all of which weaves around the redemptive story; the sacrifice of Jesus of the Seed of the woman and the Center of all centers in biblical revelation.

To deny the virgin birth of Jesus is to violate the credibility of the blood that reconciles us back to God and bonds our spirits to Him. Any compromise on this downgrades the integrity of our witness and relegates Christ to the seed of the man, not the woman, and therefore a victim of the negotiation pact (GOD FORBID!) begun in the garden and reproduced in every seed of the man through childbirth. The victory of the negotiator is in the power of sin and **SIN**, the satanic nature, is the great controversy Christ came to conquer and vanquish in man. On the cross Christ became **satanic in nature** (SIN) in the body of sinful man to break the power and resolve the mystery of sin forever. The power and sting of sin and death became broken forever. This grand deliverance of the ages was pivoted in the virgin birth, to seclude Christ from the satanic negotiation pact on mankind and give credibility to the blood of redemption for man's total liberation, hallelujah!!!!

The blood of Jesus brought a complete remedy to counter Satan and redeem the totality of man. Vengeance was in that blood, judgment followed and finally redemption and restoration.

Christ's coming and virgin birth was for a spiritual purpose and the relativity is in bonding us to God, our Father and Creator.

The point of contact where we bond to God is in our heart. Just as a man bonds to a woman by penetrating the hymen and shedding blood so Christ spilled His blood for us on Calvary and seeks to penetrate our hearts with the reproductive living seed of His word **(LEVITICUS 17:11)**. When we receive Him into our innermost, we are bonded to Him through repentance, by acknowledging our sin and confessing them asking for mercy, we experience the circumcising of the foreskin of our heart' **(symbolic of the hymen in the woman)** and the shed blood of Christ is spilled on the open wound cleansing, liberating and bonding us to God **(DEUT. 10:16, 30:6; JER. 4:4; ROM. 2:28,29, COL 2:11 PHIL 3:3)**.

The foreskin of our heart, which depicts the rebellious and satanic nature in us, is a type of spiritual hymen that must be broken before Christ can bond to us in spiritual salvation. That hymen confronts Him at the entrance of our lives and only His power of redemption can break it and let in His blood to transform our deformed spirit washing, cleaning and regenerating us into His likeness and glory, which was lost in the fall.

*"For I am jealous over you with godly jealousy: for I have espoused you to one husband, that I may present you as a chaste virgin to Christ. But I fear, lest by any means, as the serpent beguiled Eve through his subtlety, so your minds should be corrupted from the simplicity that is in Christ."*
**(11 CORINTH. 11:2,3).**

The gospel makes us chaste and Jesus is the word and power of the gospel. He uses the word and power of the gospel to chastise us and bring us to a state of chastity, relatively to a virgin, where we become espoused or bonded to God through Christ; as a virgin is bonded to one man or husband. You can only give your virginity once and that to only one man, though you can express your love unconditionally to many. We are bonded to Christ in our minds, which is the gateway to our spirit. Relative to the error of Eve, our marriage or bonding to Christ can be violated when we willfully transgress His holy word and commandments. We can, however, choose to remain faithful in obedience to Him the rest of our days.

Yes, by accepting the simplicity of the gospel of Christ, you can be bonded and remain bonded by willful obedience to Christ. When a virgin becomes bonded to one husband, there lies another dimension in the newfound garden of aloes and spices for the blessed pleasure of the man.

Her sexuality: The fountain of nourishment.

# HER SEXUALITY: The Fountain of Nourishment

*"And Adam knew Eve his wife; and she conceived, and bare Cain, and said, I have gotten a man from the LORD. God is a Spirit; and they that worship Him must worship Him in spirit and in truth.*

*For you are bought with a price: therefore glorify God in your body, and in your spirit, which are God's.*

*Drink water out of thine own cistern, and running waters out of thine own well Let them be only thine own, and not strangers with thee.*

*THERE is therefore now no condemnation to them which are in Christ Jesus, who walk not after the flesh, but after the spirit.*

*For Adam was first formed, then Eve.*

*Notwithstanding she shall be saved in childbearing, if they continue in faith and charity and holiness with sobriety."*

**GENESIS 4:1; JOHN 4:24; 1 CORINTHIANS 6:20; PROVERBS 5:15,17; ROMANS 8:1; 1 TIMOTHY 2:13,15**

*"And Adam knew Eve his wife; and she conceived, and bear Cain, and said, I have gotten a man from the LORD."*

The creation is all about the communication skill of the Almighty. Communication formed the basis, the purpose, for the creation.

God wanted to reveal His glory and majesty in fleshly proportions so He used the medium of the creation as His communication tool. *'For the invisible things of Him from the creation of the world are clearly seen, being understood by the things that are made, even His eternal power and Godhead; so that they are without excuse'* **(ROMANS 1:20).**

Man acquired divine knowledge, the knowledge of God, through what was revealed about the Creator in the creation. And the consummation of that knowledge was the worship of the true and only wise God, the Creator of heaven and earth.

Worship became the deepest form of communication as man alone, in the creation, was empowered with the capacity to worship God in spirit and in truth. Worship is a spirit-to-spirit communication from man to God, which produces a profound experience that cannot be defined in earthly terms. Our language simply lacks the capacity and sufficiency to express spiritual communication in fleshly proportions.

The creation of the woman became the force of relativity to man, chiefly her body. Following this line, God designed the sexuality of the woman as the deepest form of communication on this side of the great divide, in relativity to worship, a spirit-to-spirit dialog, interpreted and understood only in spiritual terms. It is on this spiritual plane that the veil is completely taken off and our true self is exposed in the inner court of the temple of our bodies. While the bodies are locked in passion, the spirit goes into a pact profound and deep as the impact of worship; *deep calleth unto deep'* **(PSALM 42:7).**

In the same manner God made the creation, likened to a Cathedral, and walked through a row of six days of creative effort to make man, the divine clause of creation, empowered with the capacity to worship God in spirit and in truth. So would man pass through every effort of covering and all kinds of cover to unveil the woman and **"know"** her intimately, in sexual intercourse, even as he was known in worship **(JOHN 2:23-25; 1 CORINTH. 13:12; HEB. 4:12,13; JOB 34: 21,22; JER. 17:9,10).**

To truly worship is to be stripped of all kinds of covering. Man couldn't stand this reality after disobedience in the Garden, which led to his hiding from God chiefly due to his nakedness **(GEN. 3:8-10).**

There is virtually nothing to hide when we come before God to worship *but all things are naked and opened unto the eyes of Him with whom we have to do* **(HEBREWS 4: 13; ROM. 13:12; EPH. 5:11-13).**

Spiritual nakedness produces knowledge too deep for mental assessment. Knowledge too profound for words to articulate is acquired of the woman through sexual intercourse, and this knowledge is designed to provide her security or cover and produce a shield from the man. While her body nakedness satisfies and fills a beautiful suspense in the man, her spiritual nakedness produced a cover from the man necessary for her welfare and protection.

It was this knowledge Adam acquired of Eve through intercourse **(GEN. 4:1).** The consummation of sexual intercourse between the couple produced a unique knowledge of the woman in the man. It was a knowledge designed to work for the productivity and protection of the woman. When that knowledge is violated outside the bond of marital permanence, it exposes the woman in the greatest way possible and breaks an edge in the wall, which introduces the serpent's destruction both to the violator and the violated, *the deceiver and the deceived* **(satanic negotiation pact, ECCL. 10:8, JOB 12:16).**

The spiritual intercourse of worship with God created a hedge of protection and God's shield of defense around Adam.

Relatively, God designed this shield of defense and protective hedge for the woman to be created through sexual intercourse in the permanence of marriage. God empowered man with the capacity to provide this shield. And it is only in this protected territory that the woman could trust the man and trust God through the man for the productivity of their relationship. Therefore, a complete trust produced a complete shield. Outside the perimeter of permanence, sex becomes a negotiable instrument in violating the sacredness of worship both to God who designed it, and with man who is nourished thereby. It desecrates the protection of the woman and corrupts the man with the knowledge of evil, fashioned as a weapon against the woman. It kills the pride of the woman and strips her of her price; stripped and exposed she then becomes unable to trust in any man, consciously or unconsciously, or trust in God any longer of whom man chiefly represents on earth **(1PETER 3:5)**. Sex, outside the marital bond, is purely of the flesh and physical. Sex, as worship, was designed to be on a spiritual plane and purely a spiritual experience. Jesus explained this in relative terms:

*"Ye worship (what) ye know not what: we know what we worship: for salvation is of the Jews.*
*But the hour cometh, and now is, when the true worshipers shall worship the Father in spirit and in truth: for the Father seeketh such to worship him.*
*God is a spirit: and they that worship him must worship him in spirit and in truth:*
*'It is the spirit that quickeneth; the flesh profiteth nothing: the words that I speak unto you, they are spirit, and they are life."*

**JOHN 4:22-24; 6:63**

When man indulges in premarital or extramarital sex, he worships (spiritually communicates) what he knows not: The true worship of God will produce knowledge, unearthly divine knowledge. God doesn't want us preoccupied with the knowledge of evil that is why He made available the tree of life in the garden. In true worship, He equips us with pure knowledge of the truth that sets us free **(MATT. 13:11, JOHN 8:32)**.

A profound knowledge comes out of that worship **(GEN. 4:1)** therefore, man must understand what worship was all about and it must be in spirit and truth, not in flesh and satanic lie of deception. Furthermore, it is only the spirit that can quicken or revive, the flesh eventually will depreciate and wear out but the spirit keeps us holding on and provides that lasting freshness. *For which cause we faint not; but though our outward man perish. Yet the inward man is renewed day by day'* **(11 COR. 4:16).**

The spirit breaks the frustrating cycle of monotonous regularity to bring newness as we indulge in worship, to God and in sex.

While the man is exposed and naked before God in true worship the woman, on the other hand, is fully unveiled and known in sexual intercourse.

This is God's purpose by design and basically the reason the man was first formed before the woman; *'For Adam was first formed, then Eve'* **(1TIM. 2:13).** This also goes to explain why the man is not bonded to the woman through sexual intercourse but the woman is bonded otherwise in the first act of sex. Man, basically and intrinsically, is made in the image and likeness of God. Man was made to reflect the glory of God in fleshly proportions and his body served as the temple or carrier of the living God, for in perfection he was formed **(11 COR. 4:7, GEN. 1:26).**

That divine presence in the body empowered the perfection principle but sin and corruption invaded that body-temple and God declared, *"My Spirit shall not always strive with man, for that he also is flesh"* **(GEN. 6:3).** Flesh became relegated to decay and death, multiplying in untold frustration and misery.

Christ, however, came in the likeness of sinful flesh, bodily, and died to restore that body to divine estate and now declares to man, *"Your body is the temple of God"* **(1 COR. 3:16.17; 6:13-20; 11 COR. 6:16).** Through the blood of redemption, God can now dwell in the body-temple of man as in the original creation. The clause here is that the woman was made with an extract from the man and her body became the force of relativity God would use to explain the mystery of purpose by design to man.

Her spirit, the essence and breadth of life, came from God and was equivalent with that of man but her body served a different function. Her body, with its intricate design, was fashioned to provide nourishment to the man chiefly in sexual intercourse and propagating his seed on earth.

When that body is violated otherwise in illicit sex, premarital or extramarital, it becomes a transgression of **"harlotry"**; while the man in partnership with her commits a temple (body) defiling sin she, in the illicit use of her body, qualifies as an **'harlot.'**

*"Know ye not that your bodies are the members of Christ? Shall I then take the members of Christ, and make them the members of a harlot? God forbid.*

*What? Know ye not that he which is joined to an harlot is one body? For two, saith he, shall be one flesh.* (GEN. 2:24, MATT. 19:5) *But he that is joined unto the Lord is one spirit.*

*Flee fornication. Every sin that a man doeth is without the body; but he that committeth fornication sinneth against his own body. What? Know ye not that your body is the temple of the Holy Ghost which is in you, which ye have of God, and ye are not your own?*

*For ye are bought with a price: therefore glorify God in your body, and in your spirit, which are God's.*

But we have this treasure in earthen vessels, that the excellency of the power may be of God, and not of us"

**1COR. 6:15-20; 11COR. 4:7**

God used the simile of a family structure to portray Himself as an husband and the nation of Israel as His wife **(JER. 2:2,3; HOS. 2:15,16)** He went further to explain what transpired in the relationship using vivid and strong terms of scriptures in relativity to this design.

Each time Israel, the wife, went astray and followed after heathen gods, God termed it explicitly and figuratively as **"harlotry" (JER. 3:1,20; 31:32; HOS. 1:2; 4:15; EZEK. 16:15, 30-35; 23:3-8)**. To make it forceful and relatively to the people, God commanded the prophet Hosea to marry a harlot named **Gomer** to illustrate Israel's infidelity. She left him, time and time again, for the ill enterprise of harlotry, though he made concerted efforts to forgive and reconcile with her **(HOSEA 1:2; 2:13-20)**.

Through this relativity of Old Testament examples and restoration of New Testament glory, we are given the complete revelation of the will of God and His purpose by design of how man and woman can relate to bring glory to God **(EPHESIANS 5:22-33)**.

Human life has been programmed for fulfillment through obedience to God commands. An integral part of that fulfillment comes through sexual intercourse for thereby is the man properly nourished while his body remains intact as the temple of God; the woman, in turn, is fulfilled in her relativity and function, producing and raising godly seed in an atmosphere of security and welfare **(1TIM. 2:15; DEUT. 22:9; S.O.S 2:15)**.

This will work to bring harmony on earth and praise to God on high.

Sexual intercourse is the pivot on which that body of relativity rotates and it is sacred and all embracing as worship in relation to God. God's woman, through the blood of redemption, has been bought with a price and her price is not negotiable.

*"Drink waters out of thine own cistern, and running water out of thine own well.*
*Let them be only thine own, and not strangers' with thee.*
*Let thy fountain be blessed: and rejoice with the wife of thy Youth.*
*Let her be as the loving hind and the pleasant roe; let her breasts satisfy thee at all times; and be thou ravished always with her love.*
*And why will thou, my son, be ravished with a strange woman, and embrace the bosom of a stranger?"*
**(PROVERBS 5:15, 17-20)**

The sexual drive or instinct in a man is much different from that of the woman. While the drive in the man is sporadic and given to intervals, it can be said of the woman to be spontaneous.

The man does not have the urge at all times but at intervals he comes 'on heat' and he seeks for a way to diffuse tension. No other way is provided except through the woman. This drive in man can be compared with the electrical light, which is controlled by the switch.

Like the electrical light, he is tuned on and off by the switch of passion. When turned on, his passion can be likened to an erupting volcano, surging, explosive. The woman, on the other hand, can be said to be spontaneous in her sex drive. She is, by nature, inclined to provide sexual nourishment to the man, the proper channeling of which leads to her fulfillment. Unlike the electric switch, she is the power that supplies the light and keeps it on. What determines the light is not the switch but the power. Her body, like the switch, turns the man on but her sexuality is the power that keeps him on. Solomon had an unusual but divine insight when he was inspired to pen the fifth chapter of the book of Proverbs. He was recording this timely counsel for his son for posterity, which was to guide him in his affairs with woman. He acknowledged the divine wisdom endowed on him and understood perfectly what he was saying. No doubt, a man who had one thousand women to his credit and every provision of pleasure the heart could desire at his disposal would be worth adhering to in this matter. However, under the divine psyche, he summed it all up and penned in **verses 15 through 20** an eternal truth of purpose by design, from the divine perspective, the role of the woman.

Much as a man needs water to survive, he is not always thirsty at all times but when he does feel the thirst for this life giving liquid, there is a divine provision for him: the well. From antiquity the well has been a source of nourishment for both man and beast. However, this verse depicts a metaphor that relates only to man. Encoded in these verses is the divine clause in the creation of the woman, making her the chief instrument through which a man can be nourished sexually. The clause is more emphatic when it is tailored to one woman '**per man**' (Verse 17). While it is accepted that a well sometimes dries up, the metaphoric expression of the Holy Writ spares no detail. The woman is here portrayed as a well that never dries up, a fountain, always supplying the life that nourishes the man. Even to her old age, long after the body wears out and the 'breasts' (**metaphorically, a fountain pump**) fails, her love, which is the 'unconditional choice', goes on to nourish the man and keeps him ravished. Her purpose connects her to the source that never runs dry: God. While the man's thirst for water or nourishment is sporadic, the woman, by design, is a spontaneous fountain, never running dry and always supplying the life-giving nutrient to her man.

Always, he can reach back to that body for affirmation rest assured that God has him well covered in his need to maintain focus **(PHIL. 4:19).**

The clause in **verse 17**, which tailors the design to one woman per man, calls for wisdom, and the warning in **verse 20** is better heeded than experienced. Anything outside the divine arrangement will reverse the trend as recorded in these verses. Death from poisoning will occur. Scripture is replete with examples of men who went against the flow and really got burnt. For in the next chapter, Solomon gives a recount of the consequences of going against God's order **(PROV. 6:23-25).**

The poetic inspiration of the Holy Writ calls for praise to God. With powerful figures of speech Solomon gave a message with a force of relativity that cannot be denied or misunderstood. Like his father, David, Solomon had God's ink of poetry in his soul. A poet realizes that there is order in life but he doesn't struggle to try and understand it, instead he floats on the waves and enters into the mystery of it through poetry. Poets recognize mystery and rejoice in it without trying to manage it.

**'Women!'** they were a mystery to him and indeed are **(PROV. 30:18-20, 31:3).** He had lots of them to himself, all sizes, shapes, color, and character yet his heart longed for more. In divine wisdom, he discovered that what he sought for in many women was found in a single unit of a woman but how he would locate the right one and reduce his quest for adventure to manageable proportion was the mystery. He did not attempt to manage the mystery of it all but simply celebrated it **(ECCLESIASTES 7:23-29; PRO. 6:23-28; 22:14).**

Realizing that his son(s) might also be caught in this cycle of frustration that also plagued his father, David, he documented his counsel for posterity, hoping for a definite change. Blessed are those who allow themselves to be awed by what God is doing in their lives and respond to it with poetic rhythm and praise. Do not attempt to manage the mysteries of God rather, simply rejoice in it. Another mystery of the woman's sexuality is the appreciation of beauty and physical attractiveness. This goes a long way to satisfy and fulfill the suspense in the man. This will not and cannot lead to lust if expressed in the proper form and with a clear and unbiased mind.

We can learn to enjoy the eyes, the hair, the smile, and the lovely curve of the breast and hips, the legs, without leering and lusting. They are lovely gifts from the creator's hand and we cannot afford to despise them.

Ladies, in turn, appreciate the bulging biceps of the man's physique; the masculinity of man in all attracts them and this is sexuality in mental pleasure- the crude complementing the refined.

Another dimension of sexuality is intimacy. Intimacy, in all its varied dimensions, is an integral part of sexuality. The basic and highest form of intimacy is oneness (as in worship) with the LORD GOD our maker. This was the essence of the creation of man and it was consummated when God came down in the cool of the day (a settled mental atmosphere) to fellowship with man. This dimension God wanted to appropriate to the man so he made the woman in fleshly proportion and gave her to the man.

This impact of intimacy was revealed in sexual consummation; for it bonded the couples at the highest intimate level and through this, man would understand how intimacy with the LORD could be enriching.

For the single and unmarried, intimacy should be pursued chiefly in spiritual relationship with the LORD and the benefit then shared in relationship with people on different levels. Singleness means to be separate, unique and whole. On this stage God prepares you for the next stage of life-marriage. Sharing books, ideas, goals, and conversation, being a helping hand, and much more helps us to become intimate with one another without genital intercourse.

**You can develop contact without contamination.** You can be single and not mingle in sin, single and solid, single, successful and fulfilled before moving into marriage. Marriage then becomes for two whole people!

Sex transmutation can be explained in simple terms as the switching of the mind from thoughts of physical expression to thoughts of some other nature. The sex drive is the most dynamic of human desires and under its influence the mind develops keenness of imagination and creative potentials unknown at other times. It's a pull, strong as worship, to a higher form of expression. When harnessed and channeled along other lines, however, this motivating force maintains all of its attributes of keenness of imagination and courage which can metamorphose into something beautiful and creative in music, literature, art, or in any other vocation or calling for the benefit of mankind. You can harness that pure energy of sex for the benefit of people through Christian ministry or otherwise. This is God's good purpose for the days of your single life and you can choose to get involved in His agenda for the restoration of mankind to purpose by design. The desire for sexual expression is inborn and natural. That desire cannot and should not be submerged or eliminated. It should be given an outlet through forms of expression that would glorify God, free your conscience, and enrich your body, mind and spirit. If not given this form of outlet, through transmutation, it will seek outlets through purely physical channels.

God's love is spiritual, immaterial, but it is from it all material things emanate. The capacity of that love is fully expressed in the bond of marriage where man and woman consummate it in sexual intercourse. Any similar expression outside marriage corrupts that love and dissipates the capacity to give it. God designed that we give love to people at different levels of relationship but the dimension of sex should be reserved for marriage; for it is as electrifying and satisfying as spiritual worship. The most wonderful human relationships are but a fleeting glimpse of the ecstasy that comes when we give ourselves to the LORD in pure worship, the true worship of God will purify the soul for the glories of true relationship. Therefore, you must not seek relationships, but true worship. Only then can relationships start to be what they are supposed to be. Sexual love is restrained in the Song of Solomon in that it refuses to be rushed. The restraint is echoed through the book,

**"I charge you, O daughters of Jerusalem, that ye stir not up nor awaken my love, until he please"** S.O.S 3:5; 5:8; 8:4.

We get bunt when we stir up passion before time. Intimacy is one facet of human sexuality that singles should nurture. The giving and receiving of love is essential and ennobling. The truth is that many rewarding intimate and affectionate relationships can be cultivated without sexual intercourse, contact without contamination. If single persons will nurture and cultivate the other aspects of their sexuality, the genital needs will come into perspective. This truth was forcefully related to me one day. I was riding uptown in a bus from home on a sunny day in the year 2000. Seated closely to the window and enjoying the waft of cool breeze, I had a clear view of the area as we drove.

Right ahead of us as we approached was a beautiful damsel clad in tight fitting clothes walking on the sidewalk. I took a mental assessment of what I saw and passed her good looking. Just then and clearly, I heard the voice of God as though responding to my thoughts saying, *"She is indeed beautiful but acidic."* I paused to analyze what I heard but made no meaning of it. I responded back to God through my thoughts like this, *"LORD, she looks pretty though but I see no relativity of acid with her. How does acid come in?"* Them God interpreted the message to my heart with such clarity that cannot be denied. If only man would seek Him at all times. Once again my mind was renewed a step further from the satanic deception that has plagued our youth which has led to societal decay. God said,

*"Surely. I made her beautiful and appealing but she is not yet fully formed at that stage you see her, and the materials within her necessary to bring her to maturity can be likened to acid found in cashew (a popular fruit of the tropics). When cashew is eaten unripe it produces blisters and burns in the mouth caused by the acid (I experienced this as a kid). This is so because you interrupted the natural process in the development of the cashew and the chemical catalyst in turn, responded to your intrusion by corroding your mouth and lips with burns and sores. It must work either ways, finish the process of nature or harm any intruder or intrusion.*

*In like manner, when you violate that girl sexually before time, her inward materials needed for her maturity and fulfillment will corrode your soul and burn you in many ways. In time, your inward decay will become evident."*

The scales dropped from my eyes and I became cold as an unearthly mental clarity and purity filled me up. I though about the multiplier effect on people who make a lifestyle and habit in flagrantly violating God's commands regarding sexual conduct- the multiplied decay, the corroded existence, the defeated purpose and the undeniable emptiness and frustration; a satanic cycle of frustration and pain holding sway over mankind. This again stepped up the healthy fear of God in my heart.

Truly God cannot be mocked; society and our generation is a witness to this eternal paradox revealed in the Holy Writ. **(GAL. 6:7,8)**. Living dead people are everywhere. At some point their essence and zeal were extinguished, negotiated, and a lower from of living began. Their body language reveals them. **Generation 'X'** we call them.

And it appears no one is spared as Satan presides at the negotiation table provided by the woman, afflicting both man and his seed propagated by the woman- negotiation epidemic reaching pandemic proportion pervading the realm of mankind; the decay and depravity to such extent as the integration of sexual services into the economic fabric of society, a world of its kind, thriving on disobedience and denial of the true God **(ROM. 1:18-32; 1COR. 7:31; 1JOHN 2:15-17; 5:19)**.

*"Drink waters out of thine own cistern, and running waters out of thine own well".*

**PROV. 5:15**

This verse highlights the nourishment derived from sexual intercourse and primarily to the married **"thine own cistern... well."** While the woman is likened to a well **(Vs 18-20)** the nourishment she supplies is symbolized and compared with 'water', a basic human need. That nourishment, however, is needed not for survival but significance. What we call sexual needs are not really needs but wants. The body needs food, air and water to survive. But no one has yet died from a lack of sexual intercourse. On the contrary, many have lived quite fulfilling and productive lives without genital sex- including Jesus!

In perspective, sexual intercourse is a human want, not a human need, and the difference is significant. To grapple with this difference can be tremendously liberating for singles. They are complete and composed people and do not need sexual intercourse to experience wholeness in their sexuality. Their sex organs do not control their destiny.

Survival instinct is Satan's ultimate perversion in the body chemistry and the hearts of people, which make them reach for sexual gratification as long as they have blood running and passion burning in them. Sexual repression then becomes depressing to singles. Despising God's law and commandment for fulfillment, they seek to drain their instincts from every available **"well,"** quenching that thirst whenever it arises.

Satan will give you survival instincts if he can keep you from pursuing destiny. Survival instincts are the basic and fundamental drive in man to live one day at a time. Destiny refers to the divine agenda and God's blue print for mankind, a grand plan 'per life,' encoded in God's word. If Satan can influence the divine picture in your mind, which determines your actual future, then he will keep you satisfied in existing one day at a time not bothering about the future. For it is your mental picture that determines your actual future. The advancement of protection promos as a drastic measure to curb the spread of HIV aids and other S.T.D's (Sexually Transmitted Diseases) is one of Satan's most perfected tools in the enterprise of deception. So long as the sex drive in human is innate and natural but has been programmed for fulfillment through obedience to God's laws and precepts, Satan will keep you going after that urge, fanning the embers of Eros, deceiving you to outsmart God's law with protection; making you think you cannot survive long without quenching that thirst.

He will give you a pseudo-cultural mentality that despises the moral purity imperative of God; making you opt for protection by being smart. Like animals on heat, your life becomes programmed to a cycle of frustration ruled by survival instincts; waiting for the next time to have a fix while the purpose, the relativity, the reason for sexual intimacy, a basic component of your destiny which blends with your entire fulfillment, is evaded at the summit of your life. Sexual intercourse is so filled with eternal significance that it should be reserved for the permanency of marriage. The world has bought the satanic lie and doctrine of safe sex. Our world, however, remains far from safety, sexually or otherwise.

We cannot be safe so long as we are secure. Security is the demented pursuit of all things that remove uncertainty. The over whelming odds of immorality and large scale perversion integrated into contemporary society has made our world insecure. These threatening circumstances has formed a mentality in people who now view security as being in personal control of circumstances, people and decisions which influence one's life, rather than trusting in God and obeying His precepts.

Security comes more often through chance and some factors are responsible for that chance, which are fear and disappointment, a result of the fall of man.

Safety, however, comes by choice. Safety, in perspective, is peace through victory. It is placing your life at divine risk; choosing to find and fulfill the purpose of God for your life. Being in the center of God's purpose for your life is the safest place there is. By placing your life into God's hand with reckless abandon makes you follow a plan that is not subject to frustration, not subject to limitation, to denial and defeat; not your own. This brings the greatest fulfillment ever but can and will be shaped by God-designed circumstances for your life.

Satan has perfected his most effective instrument and infiltrated into the moral fiber of society. The conclusion is sobering and the implications far reaching. Our world today is endangered with moral landmines that can destroy us, our families, our Churches, our nation. People with morbidly inflamed instincts of lust and uncontrolled sexual passion. Moral time bombs detonating and wreaking havoc on the scene, unleashing a moral epidemic of enormous and frightening proportions. Sex is everywhere. It screams through billboards and magazine, in the classroom, market place and streets. The business community thrives on its racketeering and the secular media world comes to a standstill if this infamous agenda is not glorified. Advertisement has gone high-tech with the introduction of virtually every product in the consumer world with a sex appeal. From cosmetics to cars, food to fabric, electronics to engines even seemingly insignificant stationeries not spared, will make you 'feel' sexy when used they connote. Sex has been deified in our generation and rebellious man bows at its alter paying obeisance and pouring libation of insatiable lust and passion. With a sex appeal everywhere, the world is forever fascinated with flesh. Drawn by the gay glitter of the material and the mundane, spell bound and hypnotized, the negotiation on the lives and destinies of men goes unchallenged and unabated. Satan has indeed had a field day in our generation and is reaping a grim harvest of souls. Miss Jezebel, his bride, has reproduced an army of negotiators and stockbrokers strategically planted in every male community leeching, extending and multiplying satanic quota on the stock of mankind through illicit sex. Turning our world into a valley of Sorek where God's Samsons' and mighty men meet their fall **(JUDGES 16:4, 11 SAMUEL 1:19-21, 27; PROVERB 7:25-27)**. The dividend of this large-scale debauchery is appalling: suicides, blatant abortions, mental disorders, divorces, multiple hurts and frustration in relationships, teenage rebellion, to mention but a few. Wholesale immorality, runaway inflation and household diseases and social disorders not left out. **(REV. 2:20-23)**

In a contemporary society that oozes with defects and addictions, the stench cannot be more relative. With his matchstick in pants, man goes about igniting strange fires in the lives of girls and women. Fires whose embers burn for generations long after the igniters have gone; raging, claiming precious portions of the inheritance God intended for our fulfillment and blessing.

Our permissive society has taken sex out of its context and deified it; ostracizing and relegating to the backdoors those who refuse to worship at its alter or bow to the golden image. The 'free world' philosophy injected into the moral fiber of society has created a social dislocation for those who refuse to compromise. Satan has fashioned subtle deceptions and integrated it into the machinery that makes life tick: The Economy. Every arm of human economy has been infected with the sin virus. Noteworthy is the fact that the economy dictates the governance downstream to the people and ultimately defines the standard of living. The invention of high-tech computers have come in handy, for with just a click of the mouse pad and one is connected to the alter of perversion where you can engage in cyber sex, an electronically programmed mental perversion and a higher form of witchcraft manipulation. The infiltration defies barriers and knows no bound in captivating the tribe of Adam; a world dining on a perpetual sexual stew; dining and dying on a banquet of perversion. Premarital sex sacrifices that which is permanent on the altar of the immediate, creating short-term gains for long-term pains!

The incense meant to arise (as in worship) and please God, the Creator and designer of sex and the sanctity of marriage, becomes instead a stench of strange incense **(JUDE 1:7.)** Thus advanced is our degradation in the cesspool of sexual immorality.

Premarital Sex is the single and highest common factor in the negotiation of the woman's price. All too often we see a girl indulge in habits that defile the body; drinking, smoking, drug abuse and related levels of rebellion but violating God's law regarding sexual conduct specifically in premarital sex always precedes this.

There is a socio-spiritual immunity that shields the sexually undefiled mentally and psychologically. Their mental capacity is intact and this influences social intercourse with their environment. As long as the body is kept sexually pure, the mind creates a defense mechanism that wards off distraction from environmental factors that pollute the mind and affects the senses. A thin membrane protects inner focus and energizes the body to back up whatever ennobling project the mind works on, generating pure zeal and energy. Her mental capacity benefits immensely from the immunity of that thin membrane. She develops a keen sense of humor despite temperament (even if not expressed), added to this is intelligence and a sound mind to work with. This ultimately inspires excellence in whatever chosen vocation or sport she engages in, energized by the pure emotion of passion and zeal.

That thin membrane snaps when the scarlet thread of purity is broken in the first sexual episode outside of marriage. The mind picks up a new vibration as a thought pattern, different from the first, is created which follows in altitude henceforth. A powerful soul – merger occurs and takes root in her mind, binding her emotionally and spiritually for life to the first partner. This introduces her to a pseudo mentality known as the **"real world"** phenomenon which in God's sight is governed by satanic deception; an organized structure of satanic negotiation on the stock of humanity chiefly transmitted through the woman. With her pride gone and her price negotiated, another living unit or cell is added to this satanic organism, capable of multiplying the negotiation pact in her seed through childbirth.

If she is married as a virgin and enjoys the bliss of marital consummation with her spouse, her mind which is intact is stepped up in altitude to work to protect the man's focus, aid him to attain his divine assignment, and create a climate where his dreams are hatched and bud in fruition. On the other hand, if she experiences the breaking of the hymen in premarital sex the consequence takes the reverse trend and spirals downward. Her mind picks up the vibration of loss and defeat, her capacity to love is dissipated and her love corrupted, the violation of her price being negotiated through the act of defilement creates a darkness which makes her grope the rest of her days, unable to trust any man again. **(ISA. 32:9-14; EZEK 23:1-3, MICAH 1:8-10)** Furthermore, her body, the force of relativity to the man, is devalued and depreciates; her nakedness, the beauty of suspense to the man, is lost; her virginity, God's gift of bonding her to the right man, goes into effect any way and bonds her emotionally, psychologically and spiritually to a man without commitment to her fulfillment and without God's approval; a violator and negotiator. This, and in many fundamental ways she becomes a stockbroker to the satanic negotiation that began way back in the garden at the dawn of creation, preserved through rebellion and perpetuated by the woman in the procreation of the fallen seed of Adam. The bloodline is most powerful; in every human life God or Satan will have to reach to that line for affirmation **(LEVITICUS 17:11; EPH. 1:7; COL. 1:14; HEB. 9:22; 10:19; REV. 1:5; 12:11.)**

This is the reason why God shed blood soon enough to cover the first couple with coats of skins and clothed them after rebellion in the Garden of Eden **(GEN. 3:21)**. Again, He reached to the bloodline through the cross of Jesus, His son, to break the satanic negotiation pact on their seed forever. Confirming the restoration of His grand purpose and plan for humanity through Jesus Christ **(HEB. 12:24)**.

The blood of Jesus was God's negotiable instrument that satisfied the demands of His righteous and perfect justice. The satanic pact infiltrated through the woman and passed on to her seed was countered by God's chosen woman, in the person of Virgin Mary, to produce a perfect Seed that destroyed the negotiation and nullified the quota in the subsequent seeds.

The scripture again gives more light to the sacredness and significance of flesh wherein we indulge in sexual intercourse.

*"THERE is therefore now no condemnation to them which are in Christ Jesus, who walk not after the flesh, but after the Spirit.*
*For the law of the Spirit of life in Christ Jesus hath made me free from the law of sin and death.*
*For to be carnally minded is death; but to be spiritually minded is life and peace.*
*Because the carnal mind is enmity against God's for it is not subject to the law of God, neither indeed can be. So then they that are in the flesh cannot please God.*
*But ye are not in the flesh, but in the Spirit, if so be that the Spirit of God dwell in you. Now if any man have not the Spirit of Christ, he is none of his.*
*For he that soweth to his flesh shall of the flesh reap corruption; but he that soweth to the Spirit shall of the Spirit reap life everlasting."*

**ROMANS 8:1,2 6-9; GAL. 6:8**

The carnal man is here described as one who does not regard the law and ordinances of God chiefly because he is cut off from spiritual life and relativity through the satanic negotiation: the sin virus in mankind. The flesh is chiefly the jurisdiction of the negotiation pact where Satan dwells **(ROM. 7:5,18; 1COR. 15:50)**. Therefore, those that are dominated and ruled by fleshly instincts **CANNOT** please God who is a Spirit, and only through obedience to His Spirit can flesh be set free from corruption.

The reference on 'Christ Jesus' and the 'Spirit of life in Christ Jesus' is emphatic and this is because Christ is the Seed of the woman that broke the negotiation pact on mankind and destroyed the sin virus, bringing total redemption to man's spirit, soul and body.

He defines the standards and sets the precepts for fulfillment for us in the Adamic race; for human life has been programmed for fulfillment through obedience. For this, God has equipped us with the knowledge of His will in Christ Jesus **(11 COR. 4:6; 5:15-17; EPH. 1:9; COL. 1:26-28 JOHN 5:39; ROM. 12:1-2; 1 THESS. 4: 3-4).**

God knows the impact of knowledge, that when man is equipped with knowledge he would do exploits **(ECC. 7:29; PSA. 19:1-2; ROM. 1:18-21).** Knowledge creates the atmosphere and power of liberty, and produces the impact of creativity **(PROV. 11:9; DAN. 11:32).**

God came down in the cool of the say to fellowship with man in the garden and to make Himself **"known"** to man. For this, He barred man from the knowledge of evil encoded in the fruit of the tree of the knowledge of good and evil. Man was made to radiate the creativity of divine knowledge assured of life everlasting in the tree of life.

Satan knew he could perfect the art of evil and perversion using man's mental powers and creativity, so he deceived man into disobedience, and this has corrupted the profound knowledge derived from the sanctuary of sexual intercourse to the detriment of mankind.

Specifically, this decay has led to the violation of the woman, breaking the walls of the sanctuary, creating exposition, fear, and insecurity to the fleeced gender. Modern forms of violation have spread the virus to the tender and fragile female children. Further degeneration has led to the expulsion of harmless, unborn children through abortion; a by-product of illicit sex.

*"And Adam was not deceived, but the woman being deceived was in the transgression.*
*Notwithstanding, she shall be saved in childbearing, if they continue in faith and charity and holiness with sobriety."*
**1TIMOTHY 2:14,15.**

Sexual intercourse is strategic in the deliverance of the woman as revealed in scripture. For when she is "known" within the permanence of marriage, which leads to childbearing, it ensures the productive result of that knowledge in the man and the walls of protection maintained.

She then can trust God again through the man as they continue in faith, in love, holiness, and submission to the will of God, the Maker and Creator. This, in turn, produces godly seed and ensures passing the blessings of productive and effective manhood to generations **(PSA. 128:1-6, 1PET. 3:1-7).**

It was not yet obvious to Adam the capacity to love and appreciate as deeply until God made Eve and brought her to him. The full text of love, God's love, was personified and embodied in Eve; the blend of romance and passion was made relative with a force that could not be denied. The chord of spirit, soul, and body comprising God's orchestra will produce harmony as they follow the lead of the great Choirmaster of their lives. Adam could reach to that body and appreciate, in sexual adventure, the deepest recess of a potential fountain of life richer than the springs of Eden, gushing from the subterranean chambers of Eve's garden; more harmonious than the blend of nature all around him and sweeter than the refrain of the creatures' praise. *'Enter into his gates with thanksgiving, into his courts with praise! Out of Zion, the perfection of beauty, God hath shined...* **in her (PSA. 100:4; 50:2).**

This, indeed, was a symphony composed by grand design as man and woman were created and empowered, equipped with the seed and the womb. Nevertheless, it is not the hole that makes the woman but the emotion that lubricates the hole. Sex should not be the incentive but the fulfillment of the woman's emotion; her mental and spiritual gratification. She is not designed to be a sex machine or a means to an end, she is a creature of purpose by design; a fountain of nourishment. When a breast is battered and bruised beyond a certain point, it will stop providing milk. When the woman is physically and emotionally violated she will stop providing the needed nutrition for the man's mental and soul nourishment. Her emotion is the pump, which releases that nourishing extract contained in her; therefore, tend to it for maximum productivity and result.

The marital bond means to affirm our sexuality in all its manifold complexity. Man's presence in creation's cathedral meant that, along with the creatures, he would lead creations' praise to God Most High. The inner sanctuary (of his spirit), however, made the difference; there he was empowered with the soul capacity to worship God in spirit and in truth. In relativity, the sexual experience ushers man into the sanctuary, the inner court, of his wife making them both ascend a plateau on the wings of understanding and worship that cannot be attained otherwise. They become co-laborers, joint heirs and harvesters of God's purpose by design. The harvest being the resultant **"one flesh"** union. This is true worship. True worship can heal any wound. True worship also pours the precious oil upon the Head, Jesus, which then flows down over the entire body, making us one with Him and with each other. No one who comes into union with Him will remain wounded or unclean.

This can only be realized in spiritual terms for in actuality, bodies cannot be joined together as the Siamese twins. So it becomes a spiritual undertaking to learn the ebb and flow of one another's sexuality. Our spiritual growth helps to enhance our sexual intimacy. Fulfilling the divine mandate to multiply and replenish the earth.

Man leading creations praise and worship with his wife and seed to God, the woman fulfilling her role as a fountain of nourishment and raising godly seeds **(MAL.2: 15)**. Shielded in an atmosphere of peace and purpose, assured of her welfare and security; and erupting with **love: her unconditional choice.**

# HER LOVE: The Unconditional Choice

*"Let her be as the loving hind and pleasant roe; let her breast satisfy thee at all times; and be thou ravished always with her love.*

*Beloved, let us love one another: for love is of God: and every one that loveth is born of God, and knoweth God.*

*He that loveth not knoweth not God; for God is love.*

*For God so loved the world, that He gave His only begotten son, that whosoever believeth in Him should not perish but have everlasting life.*

*A new commandment I give unto you, That ye love one another; as I have loved you, that ye also love one another.*

*Owe no man anything, but to love one another; for he that loveth another hath fulfilled the law.*

*And we have known and believed the love that God hath to us.*

*God is love, and he that dwelleth in love dwelleth in God, and God in him. There is no fear in love: but perfect love casteth out fear: because fear hath torment. He that feareth is not made perfect in love. We love him because He first loved us."*

    **PROV. 5:9; 1 JOHN 4:7,8; JOHN 3:16; 13:34;**
      **ROMANS 13:8,10; 1 JOHN 4:16,18,19.**

> *"And Isaac brought her into his mother Sarah's tent, and took Rebecca, and she became his wife; and he loved her: and Isaac was comforted after his mother's death. I am distressed for thee, my brother Jonathan: Very pleasant hast thou been unto me: thy love to me was wonderful, passing the love of women".*
>
> **GEN. 24: 67; 11 SAM. 1:26**

What makes a woman tick when she brings comfort to a man and attract love to herself? What makes up the formula for what is termed as *'the love of women'* that the scriptures in all its sacredness and divine inspiration acknowledges it.

Forever the man is inspired by the female gender as a force, stronger than the force of magnet and higher than the volts of the Electra, emitting from the subterranean chambers of her being pulls the man, intertwining him, breaking rigidity and resistance, flexing mind and muscle.

What is that which gives the woman the empowerment and capacity to nourish the man and keep the man ravished always? That which speaks louder in tones than voice and makes statements in inaudible tones. Surely it must be beyond the body for bodies do grow weary and old. The answer is traced back to the beginning, to the garden of Eden where it all started and where man, upon discovery that he was alone and no companion was found for him, tried to ratify the mystery. Man had fallen in love with the creation around him and the Maker of it all. The beauty and blend of nature was a romance he found thrilling. Then came the mystery of it all when he discovered that nature was paired up in the making of male and female of all creatures. In the quest for answers, God made a rare species, a masterpiece of His relativity to man, endowed and empowered with a relativity of His essence and presence, in the person of Eve the woman.

A rare combination of His matchless grace, she was endowed with a unique virtue called 'love,' the God kind of love. That love was charged with the capacity of Agape, stronger than the ocean current, and it created an unconditional choice in the woman for the man.

Man would learn the relativity and power of God's love in fleshly proportions and beyond that, he would be ravished by it the rest of his days. Her love: the unconditional choice.

God gave me an insight into this through a godly relationship I had nurtured with a dear daughter of Zion. It was time to part ways and search for a higher purpose of the divine calling in our lives.

With the ink of poetry in my soul, I desired a new poem to refresh and embellish the close of this episode. I specifically asked God for a poem and it came, as always, with a strong inspiration to change my orientation and fine-tune my perspective and with a force of renewal to my mind. That poem titled **'Love'** was an inlet to the heart of the Father.

*'Love is a decision, a choice among many superlatives*
*A decision when opposition arises and friends misunderstand*
*When life's road seems slippery and the future uncertain;*
*A choice when hearts are not receptive to seemly kind gestures*
*When dreams do not come true and expectations fail,*
*I have chosen to love you till the end, in winter and in summer*
*In presence and in absence, together and when parting.*
*Love in its purest form free, holy, sacrificing, unconditional;*
*Not counting cost, not counting errors; a choice and a decision while life lasts till we meet at the feet of Jesus to part no more.'*

I thought I had done a good job but God used the message encoded in the poem to impeach my selfishness, heal my shortsightedness and teach me divine love in a most profound way.

God then put forth a question to me, inquiring if I loved Him, to which I responded in the affirmative. Then He quizzed, **"What happens to that love when your life dreams do not come true and your ultimate expectations fails, would you still love me and**

***call me LORD in spirit and in truth?"*** I became mute and cold, considering the lofty goals and vision I had mentally built through the years of which a fraction has been achieved. It took three days of mental struggle and soul searching but God saw my plight and with the assurance of a loving Father, He gave me an inlet into His great heart. With a love that can raise the dead and restore dry bones, God told me that in the absence of essence and meaning and in the failure of dreams and expectations, if I can lift up my heart to Him, irrespective of these subtractions, and love Him unconditionally then will I see His purposes and attain divine perspective for my life. Much later, God revealed and made me understand that the reason He allowed that relationship was to reveal the essence and power of that love and to create its credibility in me in practical terms. What a God! I thought; to stretch a lesson to man over a span of three years or even a lifetime. His ways are past finding out. God is writing His eternal plan for our lives across a blackboard spanning our entire lives. He has invested too much in us to stop the project. The logic here is that God used a woman's love, relatively, to teach me this dimension of divine love, the force of relativity.

What is the essence of this love and where can it be found on earth? It was not yet obvious to Adam the capacity to love and appreciate as deeply until God made Eve and brought her to Adam. The full text of love, God's love, was personified and embodied in Eve; the blend of romance and passion was made relative with a force that could not be denied. God used this masterpiece of relativity to express this dimension of divine love.

Long before the fall, the woman was endowed with love and empowered to relate it to man. Man had been given the definition of God's love through the creation (Rom. 1:19,20; Ps. 19:1-3) but the woman was endowed and empowered with the carriage and capacity of that divine virtue known as '**love**' (Ephesians 5:25).

Marriage is a mystical relationship. Marriage is not of the world; it is from the beginning to the end a divine phenomenon and this understanding is a key to our fulfillment. Marriage begins and ends with God. When we drift from this truth of God's purpose by design, we fail. It is a wide tangent, and the farther you go, the wider the tangent. But the puzzle becomes solved by the revelation and definition of the maker. Marriage is a love story, but it is a strange kind of love. There is more to it than tenderness and affection. Marriage is God's story of love, broken down into chapters and episodes, topics and subtopics woven into the fabric and tissues of life.

Marriage, therefore, is God relatively trying to teach mankind about love. That love can only be defined in scriptures and it is a reference to God. You can't find it anywhere else, the Agape phenomenon. That love is called Agape, and the love is invested in the heart of the man, not the woman. The woman is the object, the relativity of that love, but it takes the man to work or call out that love and give it a definition. In like manner, we are the object of God's love, relatively and absolutely, but it took Christ, the seed of the woman, to work out that love in us and give it a definition: **the Church (Eph. 5:25).**

Marriage itself is, therefore, the man standing on earth trying to show the woman and everyone else here on earth what God is all about. It is not a love of affection or sex. Agape is the love that is called out of the heart of the lover as a result of the value he has placed on the object of his love. By this relativity, therefore, Agape is the love of VALUE. In other words, it is not dependent on what I am. It is dependent on who I am. There is no logic that can explain the love that God has for man. Our imagination cannot grasp it neither can our minds fathom it. The reason why He loves us is because He has placed a **VALUE** on us. He has decided to save us. It is not dependent on our physical framework or intellectual attributes. It is God's own unconditional value on us, freely by His own grace and will. The same way God ignored all the fallen angels and demons in the universe and decided to place a value on mankind. There's no explanation for it.

That love is free, it is holy, sacrificial and unconditional; it does not count cost, does not count errors – **the love of God**. When man does that, man becomes LIKE God. When man demonstrates this kind of love in marriage, angels marvel, and the Bible says the loved one will respond in submission. Women cannot realize their fullest potential if they are not walking in **submission**. The one who gave the command is God, not man. God chose the male man to be superintendent over the female man. It is just an arrangement. It is not because the man is smarter than the woman. When you submit in obedience to God's pattern you are programmed to be fruitful. This is the decree of the Emperor of heaven. It has gone forth, it shall not return void.

A woman's love must have a definition and the man is equipped to give that definition. In marriage, the love of the woman receives a definition: **an unconditional choice**; a focus: channeled towards the man; an outlet: the atmosphere of commitment in the permanence of marriage.

This was God's purpose by design when He made the woman for man. Outside this arrangement, her capacity to love will be dissipated and her purpose defeated. She was made and empowered with the relativity of that love. The basic component of God's love is purity. Love in its purest form. It is devoid of the vile and vanity of imperfection. God's love is the love that produces contact without contamination, of purity in essence and presence. Through the new birth experience of salvation and regeneration we are transformed into sons of God. And the blood of Jesus flows continually to purify us, even as He is pure (1John 3:3).

It is this virtue of purity ruling our hearts that makes us blessed people and eventually will cause us to see God (Matt. 5:8; Psa. 24:3,4).

**God's love is free**. It has been freely given to us by His own grace **(John 8:32,36; Rom. 3:24; 5:18; 8:2,32; 1 Cor. 2:12; Gal. 5:1; Rev. 1:5; 21:6; 22:17)**. We do not have to pay any more for it. Not even our works of righteousness can compensate for it but for His grace alone freely given to us (Eph. 2:8,9). Freely we have received it and freely we give it (Matt. 10:18). **God's love is holy**. It has every attribute of perfection and in everyway, divine. We are called to carry the banner of that holiness in our hearts and lives (Rom. 12:1; Eph. 1:4; Heb. 12:14; 1 Pet. 1:15; 2:9). It is this virtue of holiness that produces in us the divine nature, without which no man can see God (Heb. 12:14; 11Pet. 1:3,4.). Holiness is an integral part of divine love. **God's love is sacrificial.** It gave the highest sacrifice ever given and ever can be given: ***the sacrifice of Jesus, His only begotten Son*** (John 3:16; 15:13; Rom. 3:24,25; 4:24,25; 5:8-10; 6:23).

God, the greatest source of life, expressed love at its highest peak to the world, the widest object which love can affect. Furthermore, He expressed this love by giving, the best expression of love, His only begotten Son; grandest gift offered. 'Whosoever' connotes the greatest number, which can be comprehended, and 'believing' is the simplest act of acceptance.

Jesus is He, one most trustworthy, and our advocate to deliver us from the worst fate of perishing. Giving us the greatest alternative to perishing, greatest assurance and substance at hand not hope: **everlasting life**, unequalled in length and bliss.

No one can rival God's sacrificial giving of love. We cannot beat God's giving but we can make a difference with our sacrifices generated and motivated by that love. Our sacrifice is a test of our love and only through it can we be empowered with His essence and endowed with His glory

(Heb. 2:10; 1Pet. 4:1,2). We can change the atmosphere in any situation and leave a divine impression with the people we meet when we realize that God has called us to be carriers of His glory.

**God's love is unconditional.** It does not count cost. It does not quantify input or investments; on the contrary, it has given the highest investment. God invests life, food, hope and direction to man on a daily basis. His investment spans the whole universe which quantity cannot be measured in fleshly proportions. Yet, God does not demand a forceful verdict of allegiance on man but has given us the freewill to choose to love and serve Him. This dimension of God's love is like receiving benefits without regards to the benefactor. He does not withdraw His benefits however (Psa. 103:1-5; 68:19; Matt. 5:45).

It is this unconditional love of God in man that makes the difference. This is the point where life begins to unravel, where focus is defined and perspective gained. This is the point where the mystery becomes manifest and the puzzle solved. When man returns back to God the unconditional love emanating from the heart of the Father to us.

**The unconditional love of value.** It is this divine love that God highlights for our understanding and upliftment in scripture (Deut. 6:5; 10:12; Matt. 22:37-40; Mk. 12:29-31; 1Cor. 2:9; 8:3; 13;) Gal. 5:22,23; 1 Sam. 18:3; 20: 17; Jer. 31:3). It is only when man attains this love that he becomes known of God (1Cor. 8:3). God's love is mysterious and mystery challenges us in the area of trust. In His loving wisdom, God embellishes our lives with circumstances that cannot be explained and so we must yield to whatever He is doing with absolute trust.

**The world in which we are is not safe, but God is good.** We must go on to believe that, even in the presence of the deepest mysteries. A basic component of that love is faith, *which worketh by love* (Gal. 5:6; 11Tim. 1:13). Faith is an essence of love.

***Faith is a product of unconditional love, a spiritual capacity to hold on tenaciously in the absence of answers and results.*** Dreams may not come true, expectations do fail, desires are not always granted and, prayers are not always answered but in the absence of meaning the heart can still cling to unconditional love and acceptance. This love can only be defined in spiritual terms and it alone has the potency to produce the kind of faith that God requires of us in walking with Him.

> *"Although the fig tree shall not blossom, neither shall fruit be in the vines; the labour of the olive shall fail, and the fields shall yield no meat; the flock shall be cut off from the fold, and there shall be no herd in the stalls:*
>
> *Yet will I rejoice in the LORD, I will joy in the God of my salvation. NOW faith is the substance of things hoped for, the evidence of things not seen. For by it the eldest obtained a good report.*
>
> *Through faith we understand that the worlds were framed by the word of God, so that things which are seen were not made of things which do appear.*

*But without faith it is impossible to please Him: for he that cometh to God must believe that He is, and that He is a rewarder of them that diligently seek Him.*
*But as it is written, Eye hath not seen, nor ear heard, neither have entered into the heart of man, the things which God hath prepared for them that love Him."*
**HABAKKUK 3:17,18; HEBREWS 11:1-3,6; 1COR. 2:9**

God requires that in the absence of meaning we look up to Him in appreciation and love Him for who He is, not for the blessings and benefits He offers. In the absence of essence, God wants us to rejoice and bask in the sunshine of His everlasting love. Only then can we grapple with purpose. God's purposes are beyond our human understanding.

They are complex, compound and most times, contradicting to our pattern of logic and symmetry. Forever we grope in the dark in trying to analyse and piece the puzzle together but we fall far short, not having the divine perspective nor understanding His purposes. The only cure for this frustration and to end our confusion is to embrace the higher purpose of the divine calling in our lives, which is love ... unconditional love.

Using strong figurative terms, God inspired the Prophet Habakkuk to convey this eternal truth (Heb. 3:17-18). The fig tree depicts our lives in its entirety; the blossoming of which brings fulfillment and purpose in living. The vine produces fruit used in making wines, depicting our saltiness (Judges 9:13; Psa. 104:15; Prov. 3:9-10; Matt. 5:13). The olive is a tree which accounts for the labor of oil, indicating our capacity to lubricate the wheels of life and keep it rolling; our balm of healing and nourishment (Judges 9:8,9; Psa.128: 3; 23:5; 45:7; 92:10; Isa. 61:3).

The fields represents our economic empowerment, our ability to put food on the table, roof over the head, and provide a secured nest and safe haven for our families (Psa. 144:12,13; 1Tim. 5:8). The flock is the family institution comprising man, woman, and children; the cutting off of any part which violates God's design (Psa. 107:41; 113:9; 144:12-13).

The herd refers to conquest, the achievement of goals and lofty attainments of man, which forms the pride of life in the arsenals of his mental stalls (1John 2:16; Psa. 73:3-12; Dan. 4:28-37). These all comprise God's configuration of the human structure for fulfillment.

Nevertheless, in the absence of these essentials of life, God wants us to rejoice and bask in the sunshine of His everlasting love. It may make no meaning but it does make a message: *that all things work together for good to them that love God, to them who are the called according to His purposes* **(Rom. 8:28).** ALL THINGS, including the specifics and details.

We have been equipped with spiritual gifts and power, and an increasing understanding of God's Word, but the greatest weapon in our arsenal is the Father's unconditional love, which is manifested in Jesus.

The fear of the LORD is the beginning of wisdom but the highest wisdom is to love Him. Eyes have not attained the perspective; the ears too impaired to hear, and the heart too corrupt to conceive the glory and eternal bliss that God has prepared (only) for them that love Him.

Beyond the great divide of time and mortality, glory unparalleled awaits the redeemed of Christ. Everything done out of true love for the Savior, to glorify His name, will extend the limits of His eternal kingdom and ultimately will result in the increase of eternal reward and inheritance. Perfection from the Father's heart awaits us, beyond the horizon.

***God does not reveal His power to make men fear Him, but to get men to believe in His love. And He gives power to make man know His love. The goal of life then must be love not power, only then can we have the power to express that love* (11Tim. 1:7).** We must seek first love and then faith, without which we cannot please God. When our love attains the unconditional dimension, we will trust God absolutely. Faith is not the knowledge of God's power, but the knowledge of God's love and the power to express that love in fleshly proportions.

Faith must first be for love and only when we seek faith to love can we be anointed with the capacity of 'dunamis'. Love is God's greatest weapon in frustrating the enemy. The enemy's greatest weapon is fear, which brings torment; the antidote for this is love, God's unconditional love that liberates. Love will never fail. Love is the power that destroys the works of the devil and covers a multitude of sins (Matt. 5:44-48; 1Pet. 4:8; Prov. 10:12; 25:21-22) Love is the foundation of God's kingdom and the banner of His army (1Cor. 13)

*"That Christ may dwell in your hearts by faith; that ye, being rooted and grounded in love, may be able to comprehend with all saints what is the breadth and length, and depth, and height; and to know the love of Christ which passeth knowledge, that ye might be filled with all the fullness of God".*

**EPHESIANS 3:17-19.**

There is a depth of God's love, which supersedes the fragile emotions and affections of the human body and experience. It transcends the natural order into the supernatural, the terrestrial into the celestial and overlaps the ethereal with the eternal. Beyond our knowledge and finite humanity, it is infinite. When man attains it, man becomes like Jesus and His works you will do and greater. God's love creates contact without contamination.

That love is focused on earth and man is the object of that love.

It is the by-product of this love that triggers the humanity in us generating emotions and affection. Much as God loves us, He will not be limited by physical expression to prove His love. Man, like God, should not be limited by physical expression of love. A man can so love his spouse, as Christ loves the Church, that he won't be reduced to physical expressions at all times. However, this love that flows from his spirit is encased in a shell of mortal flesh subject to the limitation of body passion, emotion and affection. This vibrant spiritual love releases by-products stimulating body hormones which arouses passion, leading to sexual intercourse between couples. However, when there is no marital bond connecting two people in Christ who have discovered this true and pure love, they can relate at a level higher than the emotional and ephemeral experiences that often times hinders and limits us. Without denying the reality and force of body passions, they can create contact without contamination by releasing the Spirit of love (God) to work in them and subdue the flesh to by-pass the sex barrier. In eternity, we will do away with the by-product (Sex and body passion) of love and settle for full reality of the power of love.

God's love is spiritual and immaterial but it is from this that all material things emanate. That love which made man is patient and kind and does not defile. The capacity of that love is fully expressed between two people in the bond of marriage, where man and woman consummate it in sexual intercourse.

Any similar expression outside marriage corrupts love and dissipates the capacity to give it. God designed that we express love to people at different levels of relationship but the dimension of sex should be reserved for marriage; **for it is as electrifying and satisfying as worship which makes us one in spirit.** A woman can only give her virginity to one man and that only once but love can be expressed unconditionally to many. The woman's body is, in relativity to the tabernacle of old, a temple built for the man. The outer court represents her body with its intricate designs; the inner court, her mind and emotion where unconditional love emits to ravish the man. The veil that separated the holy of holies typifies her virginity. The holy of holies is accessed in sexual experiences where God's purpose by design is fulfilled as the two become one, a dimension of fusion attained only in spiritual terms and, relatively, in the worship of God in spirit and in truth. This is the mystery of intercourse, and between Christ and the Church, lubricated on both planes by divine love (Eph. 5:22-32). We become members of His body, of His flesh and of His bones. God's love revealed in us makes us part of a whole integral, functioning cell of a single large living organism: **the body of Christ**. And as we worship, in spirit and truth humbly lifting our heart to the Head of that body with unconditional love, the walls that threaten to separate and divide us, the world's system of segregation will come crumbling down. Then we will be one (Rom. 8:35-39).

Sex is spiritual and so breeds love, which is the presence and essence of God. When sex is violated, in premarital, extramarital or other perverse ways, it breeds hatred in the heart (Gal. 6:7,8).

*"Looking diligently lest any man fail of the grace of God; lest any root of bitterness springing up trouble you, and thereby many be defiled. Lest there be any fornicator, or profane person, as Esau, who for one morsel of meat sold his birthright".*

**HEBREWS 12:15-16.**

No "root of bitterness" refers to any sin that might spring up among the faithful and by it many become defiled. The emphasis on fornication is strong because it is violated sex and generates the root of bitterness. Love means that lives are intermingled, and that if my brother goes down to perdition, part of me goes down with him. If my brother is exalted by the grace of God, part of me shares in that exaltation (Gal. 6:1,2; Rom. 13: 10).

*Marriage is honorable in all, and the bed undefiled: but whoremongers and adulterers God will judge (Heb. 13:4).*

When so-called love is expressed in premarital sex, it only exposes the man to privileges without commitment and dissipates the capacity of love in the woman. At the fall, things began working in reverse gear.

Strange incense is fast covering the land, creating a fog of depression and darkness, generated by violation of God's word regarding sex.

The world today has come to associate love with tenderness and weakness and so women are seen as tender weaklings and the one way to treat them is to be tough. The macho phenomenon says that for you to love you must be tough. God's word has again proved man wrong as love is kind and courteous, not arrogant, proud or puffed up (1 Cor. 13).

You can be macho yet thoughtful, macho yet courteous, macho and unselfish, macho and meek. *Meekness is not weakness but strength under perfect control.* You can learn to love with your heart by subjecting your mind to the renewing process of the word of God. Today, man cannot have contact, in relationship, without contamination, in sin. Violations under the guise of love so called abound, and hurts are multiplied creating mortality.

God's love, however, is purity at its peak. True love does not defile. Love and intercourse are directly related in marriage. The deeper love grows between each other, the sharing of their inner lives, the more enjoyable intercourse becomes. God designed sex specifically to relate to man the profound effect of worship; both planes being spiritual are lubricated by love and produce the harvest of oneness in spirit.

I pondered on the frenzy that the world celebrates and deifies as lovers' day called **Valentine**, until God inspired me with truth, which I composed as a poem.

*"Valentine comes with many definition to people creating a picture in the mind depicting love they neither understand nor possess; Feelings are stirred, emotions appeased in a show of vanity and emptiness while the soul longs for more.*

*We have the real thing: the substance, the life and the meaning. Remembering this brings joy in my heart and thanksgiving for the providence that brought us to light, for time and eternity in love, as we journey on the tropical exuberance of redeeming love.*

The congenital defect that occurred in Adam and Eve after the fall was specific. The man became insecure and this lead to his hiding from God. Insecurity has been reproduced in the Adamic race down to our day. Insecurity is the direct result in a world devoid of God's love and the hope that love generates. In its absence, fear reigns. It has become an end-time obsession. Insecurity is a state of fear where man adopts certain measures to deal with the fear of the unknown called **uncertainty**. It's a mental syndrome that kills love and trust in man and makes him want to dominate out of fear and insecurity; a pseudo covering (Gen. 3:7). Love breeds trust and produces a shield; the more trust invested the greater the shield, and a complete trust becomes a complete shield. The fear of failure creates a fog of depression in man and generates fear of the unknown future, which creates further insecurity. God contrasts love with fear and gives love as the antidote to deal with fear (1 John 4:18; 11 Tim. 1:17). The fall also produced lust in man, which is the lowest depth to which love falls. Lust became the ultimate perversion of the divine nature in man and the avenue of corruption in the world (11Pet. 1:4; 2:18 Eph. 2:3; Rom. 1:24). Lust is also a distortion of sexuality chiefly afflicting the man. Lust is best described as a condition in which a person lives in a perpetual sexual stew. It is runaway, uncontrolled sexual passion, sometimes becoming obsessive and all consuming. The antidote for this is for men to learn to love again as Christ also loved. Men are admonished to love their wives as Christ loved the Church (Eph. 5:15-33). That capacity has been corrupted and only redemption in Christ can restore it.

The woman, on the other hand, was created and endowed with the essence of God's love; empowered with an unconditional choice to love while life lasts. When her dreams are not coming true and her expectations fail, her heart goes on to love, not counting the cost, not considering the errors of the one who failed her. The woman is a unique and precious being, a gift to our world, and her price is not negotiable: the power of her virtue of love. Created and placed in a garden, which secured her future and welfare, she had no choice but to love the man unconditionally.

However, the true test came when they jeopardized their future and lost the security and welfare of the garden God prepared for them.

That love went on to nourish Adam the rest of his life as scriptures affirm. Dreams failed, expectations denied, purpose violated yet… her love was the unconditional choice that glued her to her man the rest of their days. It was not a helpless love as some may think, it was an unconditional choice for she was equally empowered with a free will by the God of heaven, her Creator.

True love is a taste of heaven, and lust is the enemy's ultimate perversion of the glory of heaven. To the degree that people are free of lust on earth, to the degree they will begin to experience heaven (11 Pet. 1:3,4).

On the other hand, the woman in the fall lost her capacity to love unconditionally. She now holds man to ransom with the constant demand to prove his love to her. Out of insecurity, the man now spends a lifetime in a cycle of frustration proving that love. In the original creation, that love and it's capacity endowed on the woman was necessary to keep the man focused on God and ravished in his assignment; assured of God's care and concern for his total need (Prov. 5:19). The body of the woman was the vehicle, the force of relativity, to convey that love. Sin always works to counter divine purposes. Sin dissipated her capacity to give that love unconditionally.

Further involvement in immorality destroys and cripples her ability to love, give love or remain in true love. She is fascinated by and drawn to the glitter of the material world, the lust of the eyes, unaware that it will work to her destruction (Gen. 3:6; 1 John 2:16). For this, the man's protection for the woman is meant to be a **'covering of the eyes'** (Gen. 12:14-20; 20:14-16).

Hard as she tries she cannot retain her object of love. She struggles with loneliness even in the midst of company and fluctuates with the wand of passion and instincts. Only the blood of redemption in Christ can restore that which the locust has eaten. The antidote for this is sexual purity, for only in purity can she harness the capacity to love and give love, which is best expressed in marriage. True love truly does not defile.

With true love men can become true men, and women can be the women they were created and empowered to be, because love has replaced their fear. Love will never manipulate or try to control out of insecurity, because love casts out all fear (1 John 4:8; 11 Tim. 1:7).

The very place where relationships can be corrupted is also where they can be most fulfilling after redemption has worked in them.

When the woman engages in immorality, she is reduced to a leftover and no man wants a leftover. Men, the same as Christ, desire brides who are pure and reserved exclusively for themselves alone. However, few men have the capacity to truly undo the past and forgive the sins of a woman who has been reduced to a leftover by negotiating sex, as Christ has forgiven His bride, the Church. ***Forgiveness is an essence of love, unconditional love.*** If you truly love, you will truly forgive and the more you are forgiven, the more that you love. The harder it is for you to forgive, the further you are from true love. Love does not seek it's own. Self-centeredness is the root of all failures. There are some who are still virgins and wondering what they are waiting for to go all the way. I will do to tell them what they are waiting for and should look forward to with anticipation. They are waiting for a definition of their God-given identity called **"womanhood."** It takes a man to give that definition in marriage as well as a man to disvirgin a woman and introduce her to womanhood.

They are waiting to give their whole love, God's divine essence endowed on them, unconditionally to a man who will be true to them the rest of their days, not a panicky fraction in fear and insecurity. To give that love an outlet in the atmosphere of commitment and permanence that breeds **miracles of love**. They are waiting for God's purpose by design to be fulfilled as man and woman, joined in holy wedlock, consummate love in the sanctuary of sex, creating seed that would bring impact to bruise the serpent's head as God's tools and weapons of war are born. They are waiting for their total liberation, as women, in child bearing as they continue in faith and love, holiness and submission to their husbands, in worship of the only true God (**1 Tim. 2:15**).

They are waiting to see their world transformed into Eden through their obedience to God's command, as they abstain from the fruit of the tree of the knowledge of good and evil in premarital sex, and are given access to the tree of life in the garden of purity and true love in marriage.

They are waiting to be made like Jesus, even as He is pure; empowered with an unconditional love focused on nourishing one man fully for life.

*"For yet a little while and he that shall come will come, and will not tarry"* (**Heb. 10:37**). This is God's purpose by design and the only medium for the woman's capacity and womanhood to be fulfilled through the man.

Woman, there is a man out there prepared for you with your specifics in his mind. He has your definition, your fulfillment and the capacity to call and work out that love in you. He is equipped as a finisher and fulfiller of your creation and destiny just as Christ was the finisher and fulfiller of God's law for us, which is love (**Matt. 22:37-40; Rom. 13:8-10; Gal. 5:14**). Keep searching, delay does not mean denial; you cannot be denied or deprived. God rewards faithfulness down to the most remote regions on earth. *His eyes search every heart and understand every motive. The eyes of all wait upon Him; and He gives them their food in due season. He opens forth His hands and satisfies the desire of every living thing. He gives to the beast its food, and to the young ravens which cry. The young lions roar after their prey, and seek their meat from God. But the mercy of the LORD is from everlasting to everlasting upon them that fear Him, and His righteousness unto children's children.*

*To such as keep His covenant, and to those that remember His commandments to do them. He will fulfill the desire of them that fear Him; He will also hear their cry, and will save them.*

*He heals the broken hearted and binds up their wounds. He is the God with whom we have to do.* (JER. 17:10; PSA. 145:15,16,19; 147:3,9; 104:21; 103:17,18; HEB. 4: 12,13).

We also see a relativity of divine love when God compares the love and bond of a mother to her child but beyond that, God's love is eternal (**Isa. 49:15,16**).

Our very lives are stories, God's story of love, broken down into chapters and episodes, topics and subtopics woven into the fabric and tissues of our lives. We can only understand the depth of that love by searching out the heart of the Father for us revealed in scriptures. That love can only be defined in scripture and it is a reference to God: the Agape phenomenon. It is not a love limited to physical expression only. It is the love of value. It is not dependent on what you are; it is dependent on who you are- a carrier of His essence and presence empowered and endowed with a price and your price is not negotiable.

That love is free, it is holy, sacrificing, and unconditional; does not count cost, not counting errors. Even when dreams are not coming true, when our expectations fail and our prayers attract no answer, when circumstances too deep for understanding assail us.

That love alone can kill the venom of fear, dissipate the fog of depression and speed up divine reaction to our plight.

God is writing His eternal plan for our lives across a blackboard spanning our entire lives. He has invented too much in us to stop the project. All we need do is respond in the purity of agape, God's unconditional love of value. Despite our inadequacies and failures, He has decided to place a value on us. He has decided to save us. No logic can explain that love, our analysis cannot conclude it nor our finite minds fathom it. It's not our merit or rights to receive it but God's unconditional value on us, freely by His own grace and will. The same way God ignored all the fallen angels and demons in the universe and decided to place a value on mankind. There's no explanation for it. There are purposes too deep for us to understand. Complex, compound and contradicting circumstances that do not fit any pattern of logic or symmetry. Forever groping in the dark, we tend to put the pieces together and analyze the puzzle but in all we fall far short, neither having the perspective nor understanding the purpose of it all. A glimpse into His glory will end our confusion. The only cure for this frustration is to embrace the higher purpose of His divine calling on our lives, which is love. That even when our dreams do not come true, when our expectations fail and our prayers attract no answers; when the puzzle of life does not fit and the overwhelming evidences are odd, when explanations are not given to seemingly inconsistent travails and the merciless storms of life prevails. If we can choose to '**love Him**' unconditionally, then and only then we will attain divine perspective and rejoice in divine wisdom. In the face of the storm God will put a song of melody in our heart and cause us to see beyond the horizon.

*"We are not equipped to receive all that God has to offer but we are designed to contain God."* God spoke to me in just this one unique sentence one night on my way back from Bible study.

I couldn't make much out of it till the Holy Spirit brought to my mind a scripture to explain in relative terms.

*"But we have this treasure in earthen vessels that the Excellency of the power may be of God and not of us"*
**11 COR. 4:7.**

In essence, we are not equipped and do not have enough infrastructure, enough strong capacity, to hold God's supply which is exceeding abundantly above all we ask or think, but we are designed, fashioned and made to contain God, the Giver of all things (Eph. 3:20).

Again God spoke to me as I traveled uptown one evening in summer. Journeying beside the seashore and enjoying the waft of cool breeze, I was wondering what lies beneath as I gazed at the expanse of the sea. Suddenly, I heard it so clear in my spirit, like a still voice, the majestic whisper of God's assurance.

*"Beneath the struggles, the pain, the tears, the frustration and stress, the intricacies of daily existence; life's stretching, making us inelastic confused and depressed lie-The everlasting arms, bearing the weight of His creation, you and I inclusive; The omnipresent Eye, maintaining equilibrium in the universe; The omniscient Mind; who knows the pains we bear and willing to share; The omnipotent Assurance, that you are not alone in your earthly sojourn and cannot be left alone. For He has said, 'I will never leave you nor forsake you!'*

Trials, disappointment, frustration and pain might appear illogical and inconsistent in connection with a loving and wise God.

However, our story cannot be complete without these adverse episodes, neither will it be real without these statements of subtraction. Using these as brushes of color, God embellishes our lives to write a story complete and real metaphorically called '**glory**.'

In **Hebrews 2:10** we are given us a glimpse of this divine arrangement and artistry. At the end, God will edit the story of our lives and only the eternal and relevant will remain; a journey from story to glory. God's editing makes all the difference for He makes all things-the irregular, illegible, illogical-blend and work together for our ultimate good and His eternal glory… to them that **LOVE GOD (Rom. 8:28; 1 Cor. 2:9)**. Depend on it and you cannot fail. Love never fails **(1 Cor. 13:8)**.

God may, sometimes, have to invade our comfort zone, our garden and nest of security, pulling them down to teach us that He is our all – sufficient provider and God. To crown it all, God gave me another poem as I pondered on the adversities of life that wearied my soil. I'll highlight the last verse where the message strikes home, titled "**Beneath the Sod**".

> *"All of life's troubles all of life's joy*
> *The moonlight that shines the stars in the sky*
> *The beauty of creation right in our midst*
> *The merciless storms of life's seeming travails*
> *The quest in man's heart to love despite all*
> *Comes from the bosom of the Eternal One*
> *God is the answer; Beneath the Sod!"*

There is a quest in man's heart to respond in love despite the scorching wind of adversity when the storms of life prevail and assails us. We can have respite in love. That love is a component of our creation and we cannot deny it. It is the compass that leads us home to our Creator. That love is the relativity, the map, of His purposes for our lives. All we need do is respond in the purity of agape, to God and to our fellow humans. Agape has the staying power to fan the embers of hope back to life again. *God's love is the answer, beneath life's sod.*

We have seen how sexual intercourse can be compared in relativity to worship, for both planes involve the spirit of man in connection to God's purpose by design. The real implement of worship is the Father's unconditional love revealed in us and relatively in the woman. It is a great business that we have been given just to be the Father's worshipers. To Him, our Milky Way universe comprising the sun and galaxies are like atoms and grains of sand. Yet, He listens to our prayers, enjoying us continually as He beholds us. He identifies with us in our sufferings and tears and He is the most emotional Being in the universe. We can touch God. We can contain Him. As people, we can touch the tangibility of His Being when we choose to love Him unconditionally in the absence of essence and meaning in our lives. We can go beyond the veil of material vanity to express our love to Him in basic and profound ways to reach Him profoundly. **Every human has the power to cause Him joy or pain, relatively and absolutely. He loves us and longs for us to go beyond the veil to worship Him.**

He understands the pains of material deprivation, the absence of meaning and essence that makes life unworthy. He knows our heart cry and many times He cries with us. He echoes through the cloud to us in clear tones of compassion, *"Waste not your tears and trials. Weeping may endure for the night but joy comes in the morning; I will never leave you nor forsake you!"* Our greatest worship and the greatest expression of our faith that please God will come in the midst of our trials. Our highest purpose is to recognize Him, to hear His voice, and to follow on in unconditional love. This love discovered in the woman makes her unique and creates an outlet in *her passion: the spring of inspiration.*

# HER PASSION: The Spring of Inspiration

*"Many waters cannot quench love, neither can the floods drown it: if a man would give all the substance of his house for love, it would utterly be contemned.*

*But there is a spirit in man: and the inspiration of the Almighty giveth them understanding.*

*Through wisdom is an house builded; and by understanding it is established:*

*And by knowledge shall the chambers be filled with all precious and pleasant riches.*

*I drew them with cords of a man, with bands of love: and I was to them as they that take off the yoke on their jaws, and I laid meat unto them.*

*And his disciples remembered that it was written, the zeal of thine house hath eaten me up.*

*To whom also he shewed himself alive after his passion by many infallible proofs, being seen of them forty days, and speaking of the things pertaining to the kingdom of God."*

**S. O. S. 8:7; JOB 32:8; PROV. 24:2-4; HOS. 11:4; JOHN 2:17, ACTS 1:3**

"She will do him good and not evil all the days of her life"

Passion in all its ramification and dimension, is simply defined as a by-product of love, which inspires one to greater height for the benefit of that love or the object of that love. Passion is energy, enthusiasm and strength. Passion is a clue to the path God has chosen for the woman. That path leads to the ultimate nourishment of the man and the making of his seed, which blends with her entire fulfillment.

Passion in the woman is the spring of inspiration and the object of her love is the man. **A woman without inspiration is a woman without love.** When a woman finds true love inspiration will flow, deep from within her, like molten lava, affecting everything that makes up the object of her love. The woman in her is forcefully revealed in a beautiful and passionate way. The dexterous hands weaving intricate details of love and purpose into the fabric of a man's life, giving meaning, bringing comfort and nourishment making the man a baby that never grows up. *__Show me a woman who has found true love and I will show you the impact of a woman's inspiration in a man's world.__* That inspiration, borne from the woman's passion, goes to affect the man's world in basic and fundamental ways, creating an impact that spurs the man to excellence and lofty heights.

With his resources the man builds a shelter, a nest of protection, but the woman alone is inspired by passion to create the climate of comfort that makes it a place called home. With an appeal that can only be termed as **divine endowment**, she brings meaning and balance to a man, holding distractions at bay and streamlining his focus to objectivity and creativity.

*While her love is the unconditional choice that accepts the man, her passion is the wellspring of inspiration that builds him and makes him a home.*

Passion in the woman is described as an inspiration, which flows from a heart dedicated to a singular cause: the pleasure of the man. While passion in the man can tend basically to the dedication of work and the drive for sexual affirmation, it is displayed as *plurality* in the woman. It is expressed in diversity as a good singer, an excellent cook, a keeper and builder of the home, a nurture and encourager to the man; in all, it makes her a perfect complement. Everywhere she turns passion exudes; there is a touch of inspiration in all her hands finds to do. Passion is an essence of the virtuous woman. Home décor and arrangement can be sometimes tough for the man. He tends to see the home as an extension of the office, not a cradle of comfort, in terms of arrangement. The woman's passion inspires her to do the fitting and finishing that typify the cradle of comfort and makes it a home. Don't get bored with her quest for details and passion for intricacies rather, celebrate it and let her be.

She is God's answer to your need for defining the details of life that forms the big picture, and which solves the puzzle and completes the story. Your story cannot be complete without defining the details and dealing with intricate matters of life, neither will it be real without the pain, the frustration and friction that results as the woman blends with the man's function to implement God's purpose in a fallen world. She has been divinely empowered to define the details and this is revealed in her passion, which inspires her out of love to get involved in the man's world.

The man would forfeit the beauty and purpose of this divine arrangement when she is marginalized or relegated and, ultimately, will suffer damage to his vision and fulfillment.

Passion also plays a pivotal role in the woman's sexuality.

*"Drink waters out thine own cistern, and running waters out of thine own well".*

**PROVERBS 5:15**

While we have various sources of water on earth and all kinds of filtration systems, the basic objective of water remains the same: **to nourish and sustain life.** All there needs to be done, then, is to tend to the specific source of water wherein we are nourished and sustained. This relativity in sexual passion entails that the woman, when inspired by love, can generate countless details of sexual nourishment to the man in basic and fundamental ways. The man does not have to dominate her in bed and force out the water of life to quench his thirst, thereby relegating her to a sex machine. She is not a means to an end but an end in herself; **God's answer to man's**

**quest for nourishment**. However the degree of your thirst, water does not evaporate upon contact rather, it nourishes and refreshes the body and soul, diffusing tension and bringing clarity to the mind again.

She is not going to evaporate from the heat of your morbidly inflamed sexual instincts; she will still be there for you long after you are pacified and satisfied and when your thirst is quenched. ***Therefore, men must learn to be gentle and tender in making love with their wives.*** Initiate the move and let her be, for within her is an inspiration, generated by her unconditional love, to take you to Zion in the craft of passion.

In water, the better the filtration system and cleaner the channel, the purer the water. **It is not the hole that makes the woman but the emotion that lubricates the hole.** Her passion is an integral emotion needed to produce the life nourishing water for the nourishment of the man. Though the man initiates the act, she sets the precedent for maximum pleasure. She is fitted with inspiration to enlighten the man with the rudiments of Eros and equally provide that nourishment, a dual capacity. Meditating along this line, I created mentally a poem for the girl of my dreams titled **"Bed of Our Passion."** A fraction of it reads:

> *On the Bed of our passion we will lay*
> *God's orchestra producing melody*
> *Only to those who follow the lead*
> *Of the great choirmaster of our lives*
> *A symphony composed by grand design*
> *Our hearts shall be knitted as one*
> *Our bodies locked in holy fragrance*
> *The aroma of divine institution*
> *A taste of paradise restored*

We were created for pleasure, God's pleasure, *'for thou hast created all things, and for thy pleasure they are and were created'* **(Rev. 4:11).**

The relativity of God's pleasure in us is what we have as passion and the expression of it in sexual proportions chiefly derived from the woman.

This is only a by-product, however, while the fullness of passion is experienced through worship of the living God in spirit and in truth. The scales fall off as our spirits vent, in holy passion, to the spring of eternal inspiration and pleasures. **(Psalms. 16:11)**

For the woman, the more love and tenderness invested in her, the better her response in love and lovemaking. This goes to work even when there is deceit in the heart of the man with the intention of exploiting her in illicit sex outside the bond of marriage. She is not designed to resist but to nourish. She will respond passionately when she finds a love that protects and shields her, a love that carries the potential trademark of a future; tenderness will sprout from her as an umbrella to cover the man.

She will pour out herself in nourishing the man even when motives are hidden from her. All too often we see women broken and hapless, having become romantically involved and have given their wholeness to a man whose motives were masked; **a violator and negotiator**. But blessed are the daughters, girls and women, who find genuine and crucified love in a man, sacrificial love; not counting cost or errors.

Can any man comprehend the degree to which women seek identity and fulfillment in men and can be deluded into their own destruction? Who will set them free? Have any of them ever met a real man?

What attract men in women are femininity, affirmation, encouragement and tenderness. Man, in the beginning, needed praise, one to cheer him on the job and accord him due regards. He needed assurance that he would succeed in his mission. He needed nourishment and food, beyond the edible, soul provender. Man needed support, a companion to stand by him and complement his function. Man needed a healer, of his bruised and battered ego. One to revive his fighting spirit and remind him that he was born to conquer, to dominate, to take charge and subdue; that the earth is his parish and, like the eagle, he was made for the heights, born for heavenly adventures. Man needed a reward, to see his conquest and prowess reproduced in his seed and occupying his conquered territory. Man needed an answer from God to contain the mystery of companionship and relativity and the woman became God's answer. Made and brought to man in the garden, she couldn't care less for the creation around her but she was designed and fitted with inspiration to nourish man. This essence endowed on the woman was the force of attraction to perfect Adam and still is a force to be reckoned with among women today.

Adam could go for a tour of the garden, as was his custom before the advent of Eve, and discover, upon returning to the corner of the garden where we would term bedroom, that the garden has been modified and tastefully decorated with aloes and spices. Creating a fragrance that generated praise in his heart and filled him with awe, amazed at what a creature Eve was. He had been there all along but these inspired details were a mystery to him. Nevertheless, the inspiration of passion in the woman was a blessed pleasure bringing completeness to the man's world. The relativity of godly passion flowed through the woman and enveloped the man, weaving countless details of love into the fabric and tissues of life; bringing meaning, fulfilling purpose, creating impact and affecting life, the inspiration, the appeal, the details emanating from the woman.

Scroll the pages down to our contemporary day and imagine a man returning from the harsh demands of a day's work in a cosmopolitan setting. Driving into the park, he is glad to be back home at last, with the hangover of work notwithstanding. Stepping into the home, he is introduced to another atmosphere and welcomed by a fragrance that challenges the hangovers and forces them to a retreat.

Then walking gracefully towards him is a woman that would cause the staunchest macho to salivate and die for contact, to embrace him with a kiss of affirmation and assurance that she will always be there for him. He is overwhelmed and ravished at the same time, not really by beauty, but by the femininity, affirmation, encouragement, availability and tenderness of the woman. The house is kept, items in place and kids kicking, if there are any.

If this approach fails then one healing touch from the woman can neutralize his tension and restore mental calm. He is treated with courtesy and compassion that failed to be accorded him at work and this makes it home. Still drowning in the ocean of comfort, he is arrayed with a prepared table and treated to a sumptuous meal, the taste not a factor of consideration but the inspiration of love and passion that put it all together overwhelms him.

Filled with food, his attention is turned towards the bedroom where, beyond the edible, he needs soul provender. With his body and soul needs fully covered, he is ready to face another day's work, rest assured that it will be well worth the effort with the availability of nourishment and perfect tranquilizer in his wife to diffuse his tension, streamline his focus, and keep him going. He works under foul and unpleasant conditions for the sake of his family and to provide economic security for his wife.

How awesome is the wisdom of God in His purpose by design of the woman for the blessed pleasure and sustenance of the man and his mission. God deserves not only our worship and praise but also our unconditional allegiance, for human life has been programmed for fulfillment through obedience. The woman is a masterpiece of God's relativity to man. Even in the case of disabilities, God's purpose by design spares no detail in the endowment of divine essence and passion in the woman. **Limbs may be incapacitated but the brain, the mind, the intellect, the inspiration of passion and indeed the boundless human spirit is unimpaired in people with disabilities.** She is empowered with the capacity to bring meaning and purpose to a man's world.

Adam had witnessed the gushing of streams, which watered the whole face of the ground in Eden while the source of it all remained a puzzle **(Gen. 2:6,10).** The answer was made relative to him in fleshly proportion as he beheld a similar spring in Eve, the woman. With divine insight, he came to understand the source of nourishing water that literally flowed in the garden and relatively through the woman. Passion flowed out from her in diversity of languages displayed in activities and affection. The touch of inspiration was everywhere within the man's domain, then he understood the message of the creation. Surging up in the soul of the woman like molten lava and spilling over in strangely moving language was a force, beautiful and ennobling, bringing life and spice to all that mattered to her. Affecting both the material creation of her environment and the nourishment of the man in the maintenance of his assignment. He would observe this divine order of relativity and worship would spring up with him to God. ***Everything about the Creator that was a puzzle to him, as revealed in the creation, was made manifest with a force of relativity in the woman.*** Creation is only an effect whose cause is God. The purpose of that cause and the impact was relatively brought to terms in the making of the woman, relating God's very essence and presence to a man's world for the benefit and pleasure of the man.

We see godly and productive passion at work in the women of Bible times. The Hebrew midwives of the children of Israel in the land of Egypt were dexterous with their hands. They were inspired by passion in their expertise of midwifery and this led to the increase in population of the Hebrews in the land of captivity. (**Exodus 1:15-21**). Because the midwives feared God, God empowered their hands and built houses for them; not just physical structures but godly and productive homes.

We see here that the fear of God in the lives of women inspires their passion for productivity to the benefit of their homes. **Rahab** was typified as a harlot in **Joshua 2:1** and **6:25**. From this negative perspective and with an ungodly identity, nothing productive could be expected of a harlot neither could she have amounted to anything worthwhile. Rahab, however, was a woman inspired by passion, productive passion. The Holy Writ did not give information about her past or background other than she was an inhabitant and citizen of Jericho, a land marked out for destruction and which God had given the children of Israel for a possession.

Against this backdrop, we can draw a conclusion that Rahab nurtured her clients with dexterous passion and consideration. Every man wants tenderness, affirmation and femininity in a woman and Rahab was an epitome of womanhood and the delight of every man seeking for a real woman at a price. This virtue endeared her in the male community of Jericho and she was a quick reference to the men sent to spy out the land as they entered Jericho and sought for a base. She risked her life for the men and made them go into an oath with her to spare her and her household when the conquest of their land is accomplished. This productive passion attracted divine attention and approval, as she became an integral part of the children of Israel and played significant roles in the history of Israel, appearing in the genealogy of Christ Jesus our Savior and in the record of the heroes of faith.

*"By faith the harlot Rahab perished not with them that believed not, when she had received the spies with peace"*
**HEB. 11:31; MATT. 1:5; JAMES 2:25**

She became one of a kind, walking from survival to significance through faith revealed in her passion: **the spring of inspiration**.

Another shinning example for our learning and appraisal is **Jael**, the wife of Heber the Kenite. The children of Israel did evil in the sight of God, as they were accustomed to, and God sold them into the captivity of Jabin, king of Canaan, who oppressed the children of Israel twenty years **(Judges 4:1-24)**. They cried unto God for mercy and He delivered them by raising an army to fight the enemy but not without resistance from the enemy. Sisera, the captain of Jabin's army, led a reprisal attack against the garrison of Israel but was defeated at the battlefront.

Sisera, however, escaped alive while his men were completely destroyed. For a refuge, he ran to the house of Heber the Kenite for there was truce between the houses of King Jabin and Heber.

Jael, the wife of Heber, knew the impending danger and decided to finish the task by skillfully killing Sisera herself, and so ended the war. Her seeming intervention brought peace to the land forty years thereafter.

A common task wasn't it? The scriptures, however, gives us an inlet into the characteristic style of this woman of passion in quintessential grandeur.

*"Blessed above women shall Jael the wife of Heber the Kenite be, blessed shall she be above women in the tent.*
*He (Sisera) asked for water, and she gave him milk; she brought forth butter in a lordly dish.*
*She put her hand to the nail, and her right hand to the workman's hammer, and with the hammer she smote*

*Sisera, she smote off his head, when she had pierced and stricken through his temples.*
*At her feet he bowed, he fell, he lay down: at her feet he bowed, he fell: where he bowed, there he fell down dead."*

**JUDGES 5:24-27**

Each time the Bible uses the phrase *"Blessed above women"* there is always a virtue being drawn upon and emphasized in a woman's character. It becomes exceptional and always has relevance for women of all time to draw upon. The Virgin Mary was given this doxology by the Angel Gabriel when told of her divine election and approval to bear the Messiah

**(Luke 1:27,28)**. It speaks of a unique virtue, the essence of passion, which inspires the woman to heights of far reaching impact. It is the completion of God's essence and presence relatively extended to a man's world.

Scripture is replete with affirmation to this truth.

*"EVERY wise woman buildeth her house: but the foolish plucketh it down with her hands. Through wisdom is an house builded; and by understanding it is established:*
*And by knowledge shall the chambers be filled with all precious and pleasant riches. The heart of her husband doth safely trust in her, so that he shall have no need of spoil.*
*She will do him good and not evil all the days of her life. She perceiveth that her merchandise is good: her candle goeth not out by night."*

**PROVERBS 14:1; 24:3,4; 31:11,12,18.**

Passion, the spring of inspiration, is all it takes to keep the woman on track as a perfect complement to her man. She will recognize her worth and the divine essence endowed on her, which keeps her burning without experiencing burnout. Women were the force of appraisal following the exploits of valiant men or the mockery of charlatans **(1 Sam. 18:6-8; 2 Sam. 1:20,24; Ex. 15:20,21)**. They know what it meant to inspire men to greatness or failure. Abimelech, the nepotic king of Israel, destroyed his father's household comprising seventy sons to install himself as king. In his barbaric style of leadership,

### Her Price: Not Negotiable

he went on a killing spree, attacking both friend and foe alike till he met his waterloo. In the heat of a conquest where he besieged a strong tower filled with people who had fled for refuge, he was struck from atop with a heavy stone that broke his skull.

> *"And a certain woman cast a piece of millstone upon Abimelech's head, and all to brake his skull.*
> *Then he called hastily unto the young man his Armour bearer, and said into him, draw thy sword, and slay me that men say not of me, A woman slew him. And his young man thrust him through, and he died."*
> **JUDGES 9:53,54**

To imagine the unthinkable, Abimelech never wanted history to accredit his death to a mere woman, not even a warrior less a woman. But we all know the truth of the eternal sacredness of the Holy Writ. No identity was given, not even an affiliation, just a woman **'a certain woman.'** Was she without name or so irrelevant?

She came into limelight of the eternal record because she was inspired by passion to end the carnage in her own little way, and her effort was worth the try. How many women today has held back that little effort, inspired by their passion, to bring relief to their world and end that carnage or crisis in their marriage and homes. Just a piece of millstone created by that divine essence in you will break the head of the negotiator and violator, that intruder, in your enterprise. Sometimes you have to be thrust into crisis and challenged by a violator before you realize you are divinely equipped with a millstone to crush the opposer. You can apply that little effort, with mustard seed faith, and watch God crush the head of every Abimelech violator of your peace invading your territory. Your man will praise you and your seed will enjoy peace while your marriage will experience fulfillment as God's purpose by design is accomplished without further interference in your life and home.

In **Luke 8:1-3,** certain women ministered to Christ during one of His many evangelistic tours. They had been blessed and impacted by the ministry of Christ and they spent their substance on Him in appreciation. **A woman without inspiration is a woman without love.**

**Esther**, the Hebrew woman who became Queen in the land of the Medes and Persians, cannot be left out in the women hall of fame. Ascending the adjacent throne in a land of captivity was a feat to be reckoned with. She was an epitome of modesty and virtue, empowered with divine essence and presence that gave her a price and her price was not negotiable. She was endeared to King Ahasuerus amidst the pomp and pageantry of many contestants bidding for the adjacent throne; she shone like the sun in its full strength. ***Surely, out of Zion, the perfection of beauty, God shined in her.*** Peace reigned in the Kingdom until the son of perdition, the embodiment of evil, and the opposer of the Jewish extract was revealed in wicked Haman. Her race became threatened by the unchangeable decree of the laws of the Medes and Persians, authorized by the seal of mighty King Ahasuerus, who was being used as a front by wicked Haman to advance his diabolic plot. The children of Israel cried out for a divine intrusion to preserve their race. Once again, the Emperor of heaven manifested His sovereignty through the dexterous hands of Esther, the handmaid of His Omniscient purpose fashioned for the adjacent throne **'for a time as such'** (Esther 4:14). Esther unveiled, at the nick of divine timing, a master plan that unseated the *'accuser of the brethren'*, which thwarted his scheme and destroyed his household; wreaking destruction to his evil network throughout the land.

A feat indeed! However, it came through the veins and reins of a woman inspired by passion to make a difference in a man's world and stop the carnage, the evil decree and madness, the power play, and it yielded a harvest of peace and promotion **(Esther 7,8).** The endowment of inspired passion in the woman was God's purpose by design before the fall but we see an intrusion into this life stream in **Genesis 3:12**.

"And the man said, the woman whom thou gavest to be with me, she gave me of the tree, and I did eat."

How quick man is to apportion blame and abdicate responsibility. However, this verse highlights another dimension to the drama of the debacle, which is congenital in human existence. The woman's role cannot be overemphasized, she is created and endowed with divine essence and presence and empowered with the capacity of completion to nourish man and his seed perpetually.

Man has become a helpless baby that never outgrows nourishment from a woman, beginning from the cradle to the grave. He would accept nourishment supplied by the woman even if it works to his destruction. He is not designed to resist the one who nourishes but to attack the invader or intruder and defend his nourisher. So when the invader takes on the form of a nourisher, man is doomed to failure and death. His nourishment would reduce him to nothing. This was the case of perfect Adam. The intruder infiltrated through the nourisher, the woman, with an appeal of nourishment, food, which he could not resist (**Gen. 3:6**). Man was created with a desire for nourishment, not to resist, and this the enemy has exploited to man's mortal disadvantage.

The battle for immortal souls has been perpetrated, through the ages, on a large-scale using the bait of nourishment, both for body and soul. When man is filled with food he seeks, beyond that, soul provender and the woman is designed to provide nourishment in food and in sex. Passion inspires her to give the man a steady dose of this nourishment to reduce his distractions, protect his focus to keep him going and on track of his assignment.

To violate the woman's purpose and function is to feed man with **a slow-effect poison** and keep him perpetually a patient needing cure. This has worked to the destruction of mighty and valiant men, even of the extract of God's elect in the past and present. We see the effect of evil and ungodly passion at work in certain women of the Bible.

Adam could not resist the appeal of nourishment offered by the wife, Eve, though he knew God's express command not to eat of the fruit of the tree. It has wreaked havoc on their seed down to Samson's day. Having been informed of his special purpose as a Nazarite unto God from birth, Samson couldn't care less for his quest for nourishment as he went about seeking a nourisher wherever one could be found, in a friend or foe. This led him **'down'** to the valley of Sorek where he found a nourisher per excellence in the person of **Delilah.** Interestingly, the Bible uses the virtue **"love"** to connote

Samson's affection for this Philistine of a woman, and probably to define the relationship. No other place was it mentioned that Samson loved a woman. The first woman to whom he was betrothed was only pleasant to him but Delilah was coined as one he **'loved'**. Strange thirst indeed, but this is a ploy of Satan to reduce Samson to nothing and defeat the divine purpose for his life through nourishment. Man was made with this undying thirst that he cannot resist nourishment. Samson's quests for adventure and need for nourishment could well have been met within the boundaries of the household of Israel. Delilah had tantalizing features, which struck a cord in Samson and kept him coming back for more, even if it meant constipation and regurgitation to his bloated bowels of food and passion. Slowly but surely it worked to his destruction (**Judges 16:4-20**). *God's mighty general came crashing like a pack of cards and Satan again scored one remarkable blow against God's agenda for man.* That blow has been repeated again and again in our time as we hear of stars, God's generals of mighty and valiant men, falling out of their constellation, within the orbit of divine grace, and creating a graveyard of stars in the spaces they once occupied.

**One night of passion can bring a lifetime of pain**. With the multiplied number of women and virtues today, the thirst yet is not quenched in the race of Adam as men seek for nourishment in friend and foe alike. The rebellion of man and Satanic scheming has turned our world into **a valley of Sorek** where *'Delilah'*, reproduced in countless units of women acting as satanic stockbrokers, negotiate the destinies of *'Samson'*, God's men prepared as Nazarenes unto God to tackle the vanguard of the enemy head-on, exchanging fire for fire till the foe is vanquished, end up becoming victims of the enemy onslaught. Yes, that passion in the woman is the key to the nourishment of the man, God's man, beginning in Eden to the last man that will be born.

Satan has perfected the art of diversion and negotiation especially using the woman, to the detriment of the man.

**Solomon**, another of God's generals, came on the scene; a colossus of divine wisdom empowered to relay the wisdom of God to a world void of understanding. Never a man had that capacity

## Her Price: Not Negotiable

nor ever a man born of woman attained it yet. He was exceptional, divinely favored and privileged, but Satan would not have him stay on track.

All he needed do to create a diversion and deflect purpose was to fan the embers of Eros and increase the heat. *When the heat is greatest and the temperature highest, man would opt for any source of relief far and near.* In his quest for adventure and craving for nourishment, Solomon reached for a grab too much for his bowels of passion. He ate too much honey and he regurgitated, lamenting:

> *"And I find more bitter than death the woman, whose heart is snares and nets, and her hands as bands: whoso pleaseth God shall escape from her; but the sinner shall be taken by her.*
>
> *Hast thou found honey? Eat so much as is sufficient for thee,*
>
> *Lest thou be filled therewith, and vomit it."*
>
> **ECC.7: 26; PROV. 25:16**

Solomon became a victim of his own counsel because of strange and outlandish women he experimented with (**1Kings 11:1-8; Neh. 13:16**).

Years after the reign of Solomon, **Ahab** came to the throne and again, was sidetracked by the evil inspiration of a woman whose passion to promote the course of evil could have brought heaven down in revival if channeled in the right direction. **Jezebel** understood the power of a woman's passion over a man and she was fully inspired to perfect it only, this time, to the pollution of the land with witchcraft and idolatry, legislated with the seal of authority of king Ahab, her husband (**1Kings 21:25**). The carnage of evil passion continued to spread like wildfire through the ages, burning princes and paupers alike until the **Seed of the woman, Jesus Christ**, brought a remedy with holy passion to destroy the works of the violator and negotiator of souls and restore the destiny of mankind.

> *"To whom also he shewed himself alive after his passion by many infallible proofs, being seen of them forty days, and speaking of things pertaining to the kingdom of God."*
>
> **ACTS 1:3**

This verse is the only record in scriptures that sums up the life of Christ with this unique word, dedicated to a single purpose: **passion for the will of God the Father**. What was His passion all about? We see its relativity in the woman.

> *"Then took Mary a pound of ointment of spikenard, very costly, and anointed the feet of Jesus, and wiped his feet with her hair: and the house was filled with the odor of the ointment."*
>
> **JOHN 12:3**

Mary had come to love Jesus, the Master, wholeheartedly and she spent a fortune in purchasing a choice ointment to anoint Jesus. This was the best expression of her love for the Savior.

A woman without the inspiration of passion is a woman without love. Passion in the woman is in relativity to the zeal of the LORD in Jesus. Passion in Christ is described as an inspiration, which flowed from a heart dedicated to a single cause: the will of the Father. Prophesied of in His birth and the establishment of His eternal kingdom and government, the prophetic fulfillment would come by the zeal of the LORD (**Isa. 9:6,7**).

Jesus came in fulfillment of God's word with zeal unrivalled, in doing the Father's will (**John 2:17; 4:34; 5:30; Heb. 10:7**). His passion was inspired by the love of the Father bestowed on Him (**Matt. 3:17; John 8:29; 10:17; 17:23-26**). Passion cannot bud or inspire in the absence of love. This passionate zeal for the Father's will was fully expressed in the death of Jesus on our behalf.

> *"But we see Jesus, who was made a little lower than the angels for the sufferings of death, crowned with glory and honour; that he by the grace of God should taste death for every man.*
> *For he hath made him to be sin for us, who knew no sin; that we might be made the righteousness of God in him."*
>
> **HEB. 2:9; 11COR. 5:21**

**Christ is the alphabet out of which God frames every sentence, every paragraph, and every chapter of His Salvation story. Every road in the Old Testament converges on Him and every road in**

**the New Testament emerges from Him. Everything in the Bible revolves around Him – the Center of all centers** (Rev. 1:8).

He tasted death for everyone; every seed of the Adamic race was atoned for and covered by His provision. He has the key to our fulfillment, our definition, and our purpose.

*"For none of us liveth to himself, and no man dieth to himself.*
*For whether we live, we live unto the Lord; and whether we die, we die unto the Lord: whether we live therefore, or die, we are the Lord's."*

**ROMANS 14:7,8.**

Christ's virgin birth made Him the seed of the woman. Free from the contamination of the Adamic blood infected with the sin virus. Christ's death ensures the destruction of the satanic nature in us and the negotiation pact binding us, restoring us to purpose by design of the Father as it were in the beginning. Christ's resurrection validates God's will and passion for our fulfillment; the establishing of His will on earth as it is in heaven.

*"For where a testament is, there must also of necessity be the death of the testator.*
*For a testament is of force after men are dead: otherwise it is of no strength at all while the testator liveth.*
*For to this end Christ both died, and rose, and revived, that he might be Lord both of the dead and living."*

**HEB. 9:16,17; ROM. 14:9**

Christ has reversed the diversion of the enemy on the destinies of men and women, bringing total restoration. Passion inspired without wisdom leads to frustration and destruction as in the case of Delilah and Jezebel to mention a few.

*"EVERY wise woman buideth her house: but the foolish plucketh it down with her hands.*
*Through wisdom is a house builded; and by understanding it is established.*
*But there is a spirit in man: and the inspiration of the Almighty giveth them understanding."*

**PROV. 14:1; 24:3; JOB 32:8**

Christ alone can restore the inspiration of passion in the woman, to work for the productive benefit of the man and home. And He alone can inspire the woman to satisfy and bring meaning to the man's congenitally defective quest for nourishment and keep him nourished the rest of his days. A man needs more than the nourishment provided by the woman's passion. He needs a place called home, where he can hatch his dreams and watch them grow. A place where he can be treated as king with courtesy, submission and compassion, that fails to be accorded him at work, and this makes it home. A place where he can be healed and restored, of his bruised and battered ego. Man needs a companion to stand by him and complement his function; one to revive his fighting spirit and remind him that he was born to conquer and take charge. Man needed an answer from God and God made you, the woman, His answer for man. **When you have answers your price is not negotiable**. Only sin can negotiate that price and dissipate its purpose thereby compounding the frustration of man and woman in relation to God's purpose by design. Jesus' birth, death, and resurrection have reversed the satanic trend of negotiation and violation, bringing restoration to purpose and perfection. For those who do not have Jesus as Lord and Savior, they neither have the love of God nor the power to express it. What they have is the by-product, adulterated by-product of love, which deals with base instincts of passion that lacks the lasting impact of life. Having experimented with all kinds of romantic and sexual adventure, they are left with a show of vanity and emptiness while the soul longs for more and the instinct is not pacified. In Jesus, however, we find the life and the substance; He alone can satisfy the longing of the soul and revive the parched spirit. *We can only adulterate or pollute the by-product not the substance. This is why our by-product of passion, as humans, lacks the vitality of the life of God.* When you have Jesus, you have got the real thing; the substance, the life, and the meaning.

**"But unto them which are called, both Jews and Greeks, Christ the power of God, and the wisdom of God.**

***But of him are ye in Christ Jesus, who of God is made unto us wisdom, and righteousness, and sanctification, and redemption."***

**1 CORINTH. 1:24,30**

It requires wisdom, God's wisdom in Christ Jesus, for a woman to bring equilibrium to a man's world. A woman's definition and ultimate fulfillment is tied to a man and only in the man's world can God's purpose by design be achieved for her. For this reason, she was created and endowed with divine essence and presence, with a body that became the force of relativity to the man; empowered with the inspiration of passion needed to build the man's world. ***This gives her a price and her price is not negotiable.*** Only the wisdom of God can inspire passion in the woman that satisfies the man and keep distractions at bay. And only the wisdom of God can make the man love the woman unconditionally, for in the absence of love passion loses inspiration and dies.

Working together in God's wisdom in Christ Jesus, man and woman can blend to produce glory and fulfill God's purpose for their lives. This will generate righteousness, sanctification, and redemption among couples creating in the woman God's perfect ***beauty***: ***the inner source of strength.***

# HER BEAUTY: The Inner Source of Strength

*The King's daughter is all glorious within: her clothing is of wrought gold.*
*"Out of Zion, the perfection of beauty, God hath shined".*
*Thou sealest up the sum, full of wisdom, and perfect in beauty.*
*Thine heart was lifted up because of thy beauty, thou hast corrupted thy wisdom by reason of thy brightness: I will cast thee to the ground, I will lay thee before Kings, that they may behold thee.*
*But let it be the hidden man of the heart, in that which is not corruptible, even the ornament of a meek and quiet spirit, which is in the sight of God of great price.*
*For he shall grow up before him as a tender plant, and as root out of a dry ground: he hath no form or comeliness; and when we shall see him, there is no beauty that we should desire him.*
*Thy shoes shall be iron and brass; and as thy days, so shall thy strength be."*

**PSALMS 45:13; 50:2; EZEK. 28:12,17; 1 PET. 3:4; ISA. 53:2; DEUT. 33.25**

***"Out of Zion, the perfection of beauty, God hath shined".***

The woman is a unique creation; God's word spells it so. Her definition in God's curriculum is quintessential. Her creation and relevance was one of eternal significance that God had to wait for perfect man, in the garden, to see and observe the dimension of companionship displayed in the creation and to conceive, mentally, a vision of a companion for himself. It could not be more real, however, when God caused a deep sleep upon Adam during which He created Eve, the woman, and brought her for Adam to see. The relativity of God's essence of beauty could not be more glorious as he beheld this masterpiece of divine relativity. Adam had seen beauty displayed in the horticulture of Eden's garden configuration, beauty in the marine world of God's vast aquarium, beauty in the constellation of stars, sun and moon of the galaxy in heaven up high. He had seen the vastness of God's beauty revealed in the mountains, hills and majestic trees dotting the landscape, also in creations' biodiversity: the beasts of the field, the birds of the air, creeping creatures and countless insects all in a blend from the heart of the Infinite one who embodies and personifies beauty.

*'All things bright and beautiful, all creatures great and small;*
*All things wise and wonderful, the LORD God made them all'*

However, with one look at Eve, Adam discovered his perfection was finite for this dimension of beauty surpassed what was revealed in the creation. There was the relativity of God's beauty in holiness revealed in Eve. Sizing her up in his mind and from the bowels of perfection, he defined her as the **'bone of his bones'** and **'flesh of his flesh'** qualifying her as **'woman'**.

Contained in that body was an appeal that no man could resist, a beauty that could cause the staunchest macho to salivate and die for contact. The dexterity of divine configuration went into the making of that body. The face, like the morning sun, ever radiant; the hair, like a crown of gold gracely placed; the breast, metaphorically a fountain pump of life and nourishment; the hands, empowered with a touch that could soothe tensed muscles. Her legs, like stately trees carrying a bouquet of fruits and flowers above; her voice, that speaks of the goodness of God to assure man's soul; her eyes, speaking inaudible tones of the love and compassion of God the Maker; her heart, empowered with an unconditional choice, joining countless details of soul and mind to compose a body complete and real.

These were blended into a physique giving it a finishing that could tantalize the most hardened of the male species, breaking rigidity and resistance, flexing mind and muscle. Out of Zion, God shone through the woman, in the perfection of beauty. God's beauty carried a force of relativity in the woman.

*"How beautiful are thy feet with shoes, O prince's daughter! The joints of thy thighs are like jewels, the work of the hands of a cunning workman".*

(**S.O.S 7:1**)

God appraises the appeal of cosmetic beauty for *He created all things, and for His pleasure they are and were created* (**Rev.4: 11**). For the invisible things of Him from the creation of the world are clearly seen, being understood by the things that are made, *even His eternal power and Godhead* (**Rom. 1:20**). In the creation of the woman, God was bringing His essence from the eternal divide to make known His beauty in fleshly proportions, so that things, which are seen, were not made of things that do appear (**Heb. 11:3**). And *known unto God are all His works from the beginning of the world* (**Acts 15:18**). *But we have this treasure in earthen vessels, that the excellency of the power may be of God and not of us* (**2 Corinth. 4:7**). The woman's body contained the essence of God's beauty, which generated praise to God in the heart of the man. Nevertheless, He left not Himself without witness, in that He did good (**Acts 14:17**). The woman became the witness of God's perfect beauty, for God looked at His creation and saw that it was good and He blessed them. This, indeed, was beauty and God's pattern before the fall. Furthermore, the nakedness of the woman was a beauty to behold.

Man, in the beginning, was created and fitted with a profound suspense. A suspense that could not be relatively defined but was obvious anyway and man sought to know what it was all about.

By design, man was made with a mind that generates creative ideas and inquisition in all that pertains to life. **Man, basically and intrinsically, is a mentally charged creature and his success or productivity is determined by the creative capacity of his mind.**

For this reason, suspense was generated and accumulates as a result of the interchange of ideas and interaction with his environment. *By the mystery of divine stability, the woman's nakedness and the intricacies of her body design satisfied perfectly the suspense in man.* That nakedness made beauty of man's suspense mentally. Beyond actual sex, there would be mental equilibrium, through the beauty of that nakedness, as he related with God and his environment, which formed his work. This would protect focus and reduce distractions to create an environment where man could hatch his dreams. That naked beauty was the source of mental gratification and stability in the man, which satisfied his suspense.

This dimension of the woman's beauty was paramount as its essence came from her spirit, the inner source of strength, which empowered her to nourish the man and sustain him.

*"The king's daughter is all glorious within: her clothing is of wrought gold".*

**PSALMS 45:13**

Beyond the superficial and cosmetic divide, there was a stream of divine life gushing from the woman to nourish the man and keep him focused on God and his assignment.

Within her, in the subterranean chambers of her being, was a fountain to quench man's thirst for subjection and dominion over the creation. The woman was created and fitted with God's armor of glory within, which formed her spiritual clothing, and this was as viable as tried or wrought gold. This armor of glory and clothing of gold depicted God's essence of beauty endowed on her, as the inner source of strength, and was revealed in her character of submission to man.

She was created with the capacity to submit and only through submission can she realize her fullest potential and experience fulfillment in all she was created and empowered to be.

In the **45th chapter of the Psalms**, David gave a portrait of the ideal woman known as *the king's daughter*; a model for all women.

In verse 10, he calls for the attention of all women, girls and daughters, to heed counsel. That by putting aside every distraction, this includes their fathers' house, they should come to perspective and embrace objective and purpose for their lives as singles. This will endear them to the king who would be attracted to their beauty.

*'For he is thy Lord; and worship thou him'* depicts the husband as the king and Lord over the woman and worship implies submission from the woman as subject (**verse 11**). This is followed by the unveiling of her beauty, in **verse 13**, depicted as the inner source of strength revealed through her character of submission. The wedding scene follows as she is married to her king-husband, in the midst of gladness and rejoicing, and brought into the king's palace-home where she is **crowned queen and placed on the adjacent throne** (verses 10, 14-16). The fruit of the marriage, children, are highlighted here as princes in all the earth entailing divine blessing on their seeds **(Isa. 61:9).** The chapter closes with God's prophetic promise to bless and consolidate all who follow His counsel and live their lives according to His purpose by design, both for the man-king and the woman-queen. This is God's purpose by design for mankind and through which the woman's beauty would appreciate and be enhanced for the benefit of humanity.

We see beauty, the inner source of strength and character, displayed in women of Bible times. In **Genesis 24**, there is an account of one of God's unique creation in the person of **Rebecca**. Rebecca was typified as *'very fair to look upon, a virgin'* (**verse 16**). This was the description of her cosmetic appeal but in the verses following we are given the appraisal of her character and virtue, beauty- the inner source of strength. The concluding **verse 67** summed it up.

*"And Isaac brought her into his mother Sarah's tent, and took Rebecca, and she became his wife; and he loved her: and Isaac was comforted after his mother's death".*

Rebecca's beauty, the inner source of strength, comforted Isaac and fortified his focus, holding distractions at bay. Abraham, Isaac's father, knew the impact of a woman's true beauty displayed in character and submission, for he had been nourished and fulfilled empowered by the virtue of his wife, Sarah, and he desired this for his son.

Another shining model we find in the Bible is **Abigail.**

In **1Samuel 25** we find the story of a man who was described as *'very great'* in connection with his earthly stock. The beauty of the story centres on his wife, Abigail. In verse 3, Abigail is first described as ***'a woman of good understanding, and of a beautiful countenance'*** while the man was depicted as evil in character, the opposite of the wife (**1 Sam. 25:17, 25**).

Abigail had the strength of character and virtue, displayed in her submissiveness, which sustained Nabal despite his foolishness and cruelty. The beautiful dimension to the story was the fact that Nabal had an encounter with David that could have cost him his life but for the intervention of his wife, Abigail, who confronted David with a characteristic beauty no warrior could resist: **submission and surrender**, and interceded for the life of her husband and his people. David was appeased but at the same time attracted to this virtue of beauty, displayed in strength of character, contained in this woman. In due time, God struck Nabal that he died and David could not help but vent his admiration and acceptance of her person by proposing marriage to Abigail, and she became his wife (**1 Sam. 25:35, 38-42**). God's essence of character is described as **'the beauty of His holiness'** (**PSALM 29:2; 96:9**). This was relatively revealed in the woman upon her creation. The holiness of God with the power of relativity in the woman produced the strength of character and submission in the woman, which gave her beauty (**PSALM 50:2**).

> *"But let it be the hidden man of the heart, in that which is not corruptible, even the ornament of a meek and quiet spirit, which is in the sight of God of great price. For after this manner in the old time the holy women also, who trusted in God, adorned themselves, being in subjection unto their own husbands"*
>
> **1 PETER 3:4,5**

This is God's design and configuration of the woman's beauty, to generate the strength of character and submission needed to fulfil her mission on earth, and to sustain the man and raise his seed.

However, sin infiltrated into their lives, in the garden, to wreak havoc on God's purpose by design in the woman and to deflect the man's focus. The transgression and fall of man led to the violation of the woman's body and nakedness, which brought corruption to her beauty. The beauty of that body and it's nakedness, meant to bring pleasure to the man, gratify his mental suspense and generate praise to God, now created a deflection. Sin deflected man's attention and focus to the woman, violated her purpose and deified her body as an idol of worship and attraction to man. This caused purpose in the woman to recede from the divine track, creating a false beauty graded on and justified by the flesh, while the man lusted after and now places premium on the body of the woman.

The loss of purpose brought spiritual decay that displaced her from the orbit of God's grace, making her a fallen star (**ROM. 3:23; 1TIM 2:14**).

**Sin brought violation to her body and nakedness, which formed her outer beauty, and corrosion to her character and submission, which produced her inner source of strength and true beauty.**

The deflection went into effect as early in Satan's negotiation harvest of sin we see the impact going beyond the physical divide to the spirit realm.

*"And it came to pass, when men began to multiply in the face of the earth, and daughters were born unto them, that the sons of God saw the daughters of men that they were fair; and they took wives of all which they chose.*
*There were giants in the earth in those days; and also after that, when the sons of God came in unto the daughters of men, and they bare children to them, the same became mighty men, which were of old, men of renown.*
*And God saw that the wickedness of man was great in the earth, and that every imagination of the thoughts of his heart was only evil continually.*

*And it repented the LORD that he had made man on the earth, and it grieved him at his heart".*

**GENESIS 6:1,2,4-6.**

The beauty of the woman's body and nakedness created deflection such that angels left their first estate and put on flesh to implore that body. Tantalized and hypnotized by evil passion, the men of Sodom and Gomorrah also became victims of the negotiation pact of Satan as they reveled in barbaric orgies and went after *'strange flesh'* (**JUDE 1:6,7**). The deity that would hold man spellbound and captivated was now beautified with flesh and appraised with cosmetic value.

*"Lust not after her beauty in thine heart; neither let her take thee with her eyelids. For by means of a whorish woman a man is reduced to a piece of bread: and the adulteress will hunt for the precious life. Let not thine heart decline to her ways, go not astray in her paths. For she hath cast down many wounded; yea, many strong men have been slain by her. Her house is the way to hell, going down to the chambers of death".*

**PROVERBS 6:25, 26; 7:25-27.**

Satan has deified the woman's body to produce a false beauty, creating a deflection in man. Using the negotiable instrument of lust and illicit sex, he has perfected the art of deflection in mankind. Spilling over in generations after the Garden of Eden, the vast army of satanic negotiators and stockbrokers in women are reaping a bizarre harvest on earth. Turning God's stars into black holes, agents by which men fall form the orbit of divine grace through the sin of the flesh, chiefly immorality. Sin is Satan's negotiable instrument in every life where it is found. And any accomplice to sin, or tempter, is a negotiator and stockbroker of the sin virus **(Prov.1: 10;Rom.1: 32)**. In Genesis 12 we find the account of **Abraham** in Egypt. The congenital defect of man's fall had taken root in Abraham's heart but the deflection of the woman's purpose became obvious when he conspired with his wife, Sarah, to lie to the inhabitants of Egypt that she was his sister, even before they got to the borders of Egypt. This deflection was hinged on Sarah's cosmetic appeal and beauty, which made Abraham fear for his life. The result could not be otherwise, as Pharaoh, king of Egypt, became a victim of God's plagues as a result of the deflective beauty of the woman Sarah (**GEN. 12:10-20**).

Furthermore, Abraham journeyed south ward to a land called Gerar and settled there. The deflection epidemic was far from being over as Abimelech, king of Gerar, sent and took Sarah after confirming that she was Abraham's sister not his wife. However, there is no ignorance or hiding place in the realm of the spirit as God passed a verdict of death and imposed sanctions on the household of Abimelech appearing to Abimelech in a dream.

Consequently, Abimelech returned Abraham's wife to him after God appeared to him and warned him to restore Sarah to Abraham(**GEN. 20:1-16**).

The congenital defect of sin, transferred through blood at conception and childbirth, was reproduced in **Isaac,** Abraham's son. The deflection however, came at the time when Isaac was married to his beautiful bride **Rebecca.** He went down to the land of the Philistines, to Gerar, where Abimelech still ruled. However, Abimelech had learned his lesson and would not trespass with another man's wife but upon inquiry, Isaac told about Rebecca being his sister. Though accepted by him, Abimelech discovered otherwise one day, as Isaac got involved with Rebecca in a manner that was not typical of a blood relationship between brother and sister. Isaac had lied and the deflection could have been escalated but for the intervention of Abimelech who made a public announcement that they were married, thereby isolating Rebecca from violation of any other man (**GEN. 26:1-11**).

**David's** woes became multiplied when he entered the deflection track of a woman. Described as *"very beautiful to look upon"*, David sized up the naked body of a beauty called Bathsheba as she took her bath. The mental equation proved deflective, *as it did not generate praise to God or enhance mental creativity in David* but resulted in adultery, murder, pregnancy and multiplied woes spilling over in the house of David, king of Israel .**2 SAM. 11.**

Reproduced in his son, **Solomon**, the deflection took a quantum leap as Solomon, empowered with divine wisdom and understanding above all men, was side-tracked in his destiny and purpose owing to the multiplied deflection in multiplied amount of women (**1 KINGS 11:1-4; NEH. 13:26).**

> *"Did not Solomon King of Israel sin by these things? Yet among many nations there was not king like him, who was beloved by his God, and God made him king over all Israel: nevertheless even him did outlandish women cause to sin"*
> **NEHEMIAH 13:26.**

**Samson**, another of God's generals, was not spared in the track of deflection created by the fallen beauty of the woman. He was demoted from his rank, cut short from his mission and fell like a star from orbit. **Christ** charged the Pharisees of His day with the sin of deflecting God's plan for the lives of people by beautifying the exterior, in lieu of inner purity, and creating attraction to the detriment of lives and purposes.

> *"Woe unto you, scribes and Pharisees, hypocrites! For ye are like unto whited sepulchres, which indeed appear beautiful outward, but are within full of dead men's bones, and of all uncleanness.*
> *Even so ye outwardly appear righteous unto men, but within ye are full of hypocrisy and iniquity.*
> *While we look not at the things which are seen, but at the things which are not seen: for the things which are seen are temporal: but the things which are not seen are eternal".*
> **MATT. 23:27, 28; 2 COR. 4:18.**

Satan's ultimate perversion of the beauty of holiness is sin.

Scriptures affirm that, as Lucifer, he was the son of the morning. His creation was the summation or peak of God's purpose by design, for he was **full of wisdom and perfect in beauty.**

His beauty was surpassing as EVERY precious stone went in as raw material to make him a masterpiece of Omniscient skill; the dexterous hands of the Almighty. He was a resident of the mountain of God, depicting Zion, God's seat of holiness and fire of His purity. He was perfect in all his ways from creation till **INIQUITY** (Sin) was found in him. How did sin generate in him and infiltrate into God's presence? By reason of his beauty and quintessential brightness.

*"Thou sealest up the sum, full of wisdom, and perfect in beauty. Thine heart was lifted up because of thy beauty, and thou hast corrupted thy wisdom by reason of thy brightness..." for thou hast said in thine heart, I will ascend into heaven, I will exalt my throne above the stars of God..."*

**EZEK 28:12-18; ISA. 14:12-16.**

Lucifer's beauty generated pride in him and created a deflection that turned the light and the glory back to himself rather than generating worship to God. This led to the corruption of the beauty and wisdom of God in him as purpose could no longer radiate, making him **a burned out star, a black hole** reserved for the graveyard of stars (**JUDE 1:13**).

In his fallen state, Satan still appears as an angel of light but only as a cover to corrupt the beauty of God's holiness in man and lead him further into sin **(2 COR. 11; 14, 15). SIN** became the ultimate satanic nature.

From the garden, the woman became the target of violation for she was made with the relativity of God's beauty and her essence generated the strength of holiness and character needed to fulfil God's purpose for her on earth, which centres on the man. All Satan needed do to create deflection and wreak havoc to God's purpose was to infect the couple with the satanic nature of the sin virus. This would corrupt the woman's beauty, leading to the deflection of the man's focus on God and his assignment, and turn the focus to her.

**Consequently, she will experience burn out, like Lucifer, as purpose no longer will radiate leaving her deformed in beauty and stripped of strength and virtue.** This would displace her out of God's orbit, making her a black hole, a wondering star in burned out space.

*"Raging waves of the sea, forming out their own shame; wondering stars, to whom is reserved the blackness of darkness forever".*

**JUDE 1: 13.**

This deflection has reverberated through the ages to our day unabated. Just as Lucifer appears as an angel of light, the woman's beauty, after the fall, can be said to be a flash; a quick burst of light that appears in a moment's instance and disappears. It dazzles for a moment, showy and gaudy, but is soon gone forever leaving no trace of its impact. It pacifies but does not satisfy, it thrills but then it deflects and if you go for it you will be gone for it.

The Bible compares the flashes of corrupted beauty to ashes and only Christ can restore to us the dashes of holiness that gives God's beauty for ashes (**ISA. 61:3**).

*"For all flesh is as grass, and all the glory of man as the flower of the grass. The grass withereth, and the flower thereof falleth away".*
**1 PETER 1: 24.**

The woman's body, in its fallen state, has been deified by Satan that our world now places premium on superficial beauty. Cosmetic value has replaced divine virtue of character, which produces inner strength, and the deflection cannot be more relative in our generation as we see our world immersed in the flash and phantom of the vile and superficial beauty of the woman which has lead to moral breakdown and ineptitude. That corrupted beauty of the woman is still on the deflection track as the sons of God are being displaced out of the orbit of divine grace like it was in the beginning when the sons of God saw the daughters of men that they were fair and took them; not keeping their first estate but left their own habitation
**GEN. 6:1-5; JUDE 1:6.**

The light of God's glory and its relativity in the woman is now turned back to herself rather than generating worship to God. Besides the corruption of her beauty and loss of purpose, the result of her negotiation and violation is appalling. The cry for women liberation, women emancipation and women rights abound and echoes the world over today, which has become the refrain of an afflicted gender in a cursed world. God's word cannot be more therapeutic as the refrain of God's redemptive measure has sounded from the time of old.

*"But let it be the hidden man of the heart, in that which is not corruptible even the ornament of a meek and quiet spirit, which is in the sight of God of great price".*
**1 PETER 3:4.**

The clamor and cry of the afflicted feminine gender would be answered if she would look to the source and center of her purpose. She was created and endowed with an ornament of God's essence, His presence and relativity, of a meek and quiet spirit which empowers her with a price and her price is not negotiable; of great price. Through the therapy of the cross of Jesus, God has taken the woman's beauty beyond the superficial and cosmetic divide to her spirit, the inner source of strength and character, endowed and empowered with the beauty of His holiness. Holiness then becomes not just a doctrine but the empowerment of the woman's essence and presence, the endowment of her price, which is in the sight of God of great price. It carries the trademark of a meek and quiet spirit and chiefly manifests in her character of submission to her husband.

Meekness is not weakness but strength under perfect control. Meekness is God's therapeutic for the satanic violation and deflection of the woman's corrupted beauty, which has left her with conceited and bloated bowels of ego and inordinate ambition, clamoring for recognition, which has become the anthem of a fleeced gender in our world today. The inner strength of meekness creates submission, which generates a beauty that places her back to God's orbit to end the violation and restore her purpose for creation. It is the lack of this virtue that has led to the victimization and violation of the woman, which has generated the clamor for equal rights and protection for women. Sin has stripped her of her price and honour while the negotiation and violation goes unabated. But we have this treasure in earthen vessels, that the Excellency of the power may be of God and not of us (2 COR. 4:7).

That no flesh should glory in His presence (1 COR. 1:29).

God has stripped flesh of the satanic deflection and given us perspective. The effect of the fall has been reduced and will loose its grip on us, when we see the vileness and ugliness of corrupted flesh. It is now the residue in that flesh, the spiritual essence, that calls for attention. God has put His spirit in us to work out the divine nature that will glorify Him and bring us to fulfillment in all we were created for, and empowered to be.

God's therapy was designed to deal with the negotiator and violator and bring an end to the carnage. Jesus, the seed of the woman, who is described as the Rose of Sharon, the Purifier and chiefest among ten thousand, became marred in his visage and beauty to bring redemption for mankind (S.O.S. 2:1, MAL 3:3, S.O.S. 5:10).

Christ descended to the valley of depression (earth) where mankind, fallen from God's orbit of grace plunged and there He became the lily of the valley to us (S.O.S. 2:1).

*"As many were astonied at thee; his visage was so marred more than any man, and his form more than the sons of men; for he shall grow up before him as a tender plant, and as a root out of a dry ground; he hath no form nor comeliness; and when we shall see him, there is no beauty that we should desire him. He is despised and rejected of men; a man of sorrows, and acquainted with grief; and we hid as it were our faces from him; he was despised, and we esteemed him not.*

*Surely he hath born our grief, and carried our sorrows; yet we did esteem him stricken, smitten of God, and afflicted. But he was wounded for our transgressions, he was busied for our iniquities; the chastisement of our peace was upon him, and with his stripes we are healed"*

**ISAIAH 52:14; 53:2-5.**

Jesus brought restoration to God's beautiful but wreaked creation, marred by sin. The satanic nature corrupted the beauty of God in mankind creating such deflection and violation and wreaking such havoc that man became satanic in nature. The blood of redemption, however, became God's negotiable instrument and therapeutic for the restoration of beauty back to creation.

*"To appoint unto them that mourn in Zion, to give unto them beauty for ashes, the oil of joy for mourning, the garment of praise for the spirit of heaviness; that they might be called trees of righteousness, the planting of the LORD, that he might be glorified".*

**ISAIAH 61:3.**

SALVATION through Jesus is the only way out the remedy for mankind. So long as the woman remains lost in sin, the man's purpose would remain defeated, his focus deflected and his mission dead. The man as well the woman need God's salvation and restoration to meet God's approval and purpose by design.

Even in Zion, the city of God, the wails of the afflicted went up and Jesus came in response to that cry to give beauty for ashes, the oil of joy for mourning and the garment of praise for the spirit of heaviness that afflict the lot of mankind. God made us, in His relativity, as trees of righteousness; the planting of the LORD, ensuring that the fruit of righteousness remain for our benefit so long as the trees abound. Satan came into God's garden, Eden, with the sickle of sin and launched a mass deforestation agenda through the negotiation pact, attacking even the seeds of Zion yet unborn.

*"The LORD doth build up Jerusalem: he gathereth together the outcasts of Israel. He healeth the broken in heart, and bindeth up their wounds. For the LORD taketh pleasure in his people: he will beauty the meek with salvation".*

**PSALM 147:2, 3; 149:4.**

Jesus came to set the captives free, from sin and its effect, and destroy the negotiation pact. Jesus heals the broken hearted and binds up their wounds with the balm of His saving grace in the blood of redemption. He beautifies the meek of the restored creation with His salvation (PSALM 90:17). The violation has held sway for too long a season while the hurt of mankind has multiplied. The conclusion is sobering and the implications far reaching; the woman stands out a target in the carnage of satanic wrath. She is been deprived, battered, socially relegated, dislocated and displaced out of orbit; mentally disrobed of her honour and dignity and spiritually disvirgined of her destiny and eternal relevance. The negotiation, the hurt and cry of an abused and violated world, with moral epidemic reaching enormous and frightening proportions, created by the deflection of the woman's beauty through sin. 'And they that use this world, as not abusing it: for the fashion of this world passeth away' (1 COR. 7:31).

*'For this purpose the Son of God was manifested that he might destroy the works of the devil'*

**1 JOHN 3:8.**

Jesus alone has the key and answer to restoration of order and elimination of chaos in our world. He defines the terms and sets the precedent for our entire fulfillment and only through obedience on our part can we embrace purpose again. For human life has been programmed for fulfillment through obedience to God's commands.

*"LIKEWISE, ye wives, be in subjection to your own husbands; that, if any obey not the word, they also may without the word be won by the conduct of the wives;*
*While they behold your chaste conduct coupled with fear.*
*Whose adorning let it not be that outward adorning of plaiting the hair, and of wearing of gold, or of putting on of apparel; But let it be the hidden man of the heart, in that which is not corruptible, even the ornament of a meek and quiet spirit, which is in the sight of God of great price.*
*For after this manner in the old time the holy women also, who trusted in God, adorned themselves, being in subjection to their own husbands;*
*Even as Sarah obeyed Abraham, calling him lord whose daughter ye are, as long as ye do well, and are not afraid with any amazement.*
*Likewise, ye husbands, dwell with them according to knowledge, giving honor unto the wife, as unto the weaker vessels, and as being heirs together of the grace of life; that your prayers be not hindered".*

**1 PETER 3:1-7.**

Christ here is setting the precedent for our fulfillment, as humans, and showing how man and woman can relate to bring glory to God and fulfil God's purpose by design on earth; His will being done on earth as it is in heaven. The first precedent for fulfillment goes to the woman and it calls for her submission to her husband, not a passive allegiance but an active rest. However beauty is generated by her inner source of strength which is the ornament of a meek and quiet spirit and which is in the sight of God of great price (verse 4). The king's daughter is all glorious within; her clothing (ornament) is of wrought gold (PSALM 45:13). Holiness is the empowerment of the woman's essence and honour of her presence; the endowment of her price which manifests chiefly in her character of submission to her husband. Even when the husband does not have the salvation of Jesus in his life's he can be won through the virtue of submission emitting from the woman. She becomes God's word made flesh and relative to the man's need for God's restoration and support (JOHN 1:14) God chose the Adamic male to be superintendent over the Adamic female not because the man is smarter than the woman. It is just an arrangement, God's configuration of purpose by design to bring glory to His name. Women cannot realize their fullest potential if they are not walking in SUBMISSION. The one who gave the command is God, not man. When you submit in obedience to God's pattern you are programmed to be FRUITFUL.

Furthermore, God does not condemn the use of cosmetic appeal that appraises the looks of women but is calling for perspective and objectivity in that which is lasting; that which goes beyond the superficial to the spirit, beyond time to eternity and eternal relevance (1 TIM. 2:9). Our greatest reward and fulfillment is to gain God's approval not man's appraisal. Christ restores the woman's beauty in the inner strength of character, which resonates chiefly in her submission (EPH. 5:22-24).

*"And Adam was not deceived, but the woman being deceived was in the transgression.*
*Notwithstanding, she shall be saved in childbearing, if they continue in faith and charity and holiness with sobriety".*

**1 TIMOTHY 2:14, 15.**

The woman's clamor for equal rights with man violates submission and dissipates purpose by design. This is Satan's subtle attempt to keep the woman perpetually deceived and sidetracked, impeach her divine credibility, negotiate her price and destroy the domestic monument that works for fulfillment and to God's glory.

Whenever the Bible mentions holiness in connection with women, it always centres on submission to a higher authority, either to her father or her husband. Man represents God on earth and the woman is specifically told to submit to the man 'AS' unto the Lord in recognition that the husband is the head of the wife As Christ is the head of the church and Savior of the body. The reciprocal of this to the woman is the love of her husband invested in her (EPH. 5:25, 28, 33). This is God's purpose by design and the harvest becomes our fulfillment in 'that He might be glorified' (ISA. 61:3).

*"GREAT is the LORD, and greatly to be praised in the city of our God, in the mountain of his holiness.*
*Beautiful for situation, the joy of the whole earth is mount Zion, on the sides of the north, the city of the great king.*
*They go from strength to strength, every one of them in Zion appeareth before GOD".*
**PSALMS 48:1,2; 84:5-7.**

'Beautiful for situation' speaks of the location or siting of God's mountain of holiness symbolically referring to Zion. And we, the church of God and body of Christ, are God's Zion (HEB. 12:22; PSALM 84:5-7; 87:1-3).

His holiness becomes our source of strength, as we trust in Him (PSALM 46: 1; 84:5-7; 110:3; PROV. 10:29).

*"With the ancient is wisdom; and in length of days understanding. With him is wisdom and strength, he hath counsel and understanding. Trust ye in the LORD forever; for in the LORD JEHOVAH is everlasting strength.*
*Seek the LORD, and his strength; seek his face evermore".*
**JOB 12:12, 13; ISA. 26:4: PSALM 105:4**

David was qualified with the adjective 'beautiful; because his life was built on trust in God which became the source of his strength **(1 SAM 16:12, 18; PSLAM 28:7, 8).** God is our everlasting strength and source of beauty. Relatively, in the woman, God empowers her essence and presence with the virtue of holiness, the strength of character and submission, which gives her a price and her price is not negotiable. "How beautiful are thy feet with shoes, O prince's daughter! The joints of thy thighs are like jewels the worked of the hands of a cunning workman.

Thy shoes shall be iron and brass; and as thy days, so shall thy strength be".

## S. O. S. 7:1, DEUT. 33:25.

The divine creator, with the dextrous skills of Omnipotence, fashioned the woman, likened to the work of a cunning workman, and gave her the shoes of submission, made of iron and brass, capable of trudging through the terrain of a dark world in the journey of life's years.

Beauty tends to fade and wither in the scorching sun of age but when it comes from the inner source of submission, God's endowment of virtue and character, 'as your days so shall your strength be'. Someday you will, shod with the shoes of iron and brass, walk into the presence of His glory, the imperial throne of the Almighty, with exceeding joy and gladness. For when you have gone the last mile of the way, you will rest at the close of the day, assured that joy awaits you, at the last mile of the way.

*"Favor is deceitful, and beauty is vain: but a woman that feareth the LORD, she shall be praised".*

**PROVERBS 31:30.**

The fear of the LORD is the beginning of wisdom but the highest wisdom is to love God and embrace His ways. The beauty of His holiness is our inner source of strength and it's relativity we see expressed through the woman in character and submission. She is but a vessel of the divine essence of beauty and this essence is empowered by **her virtue: the divine endowment.**

# HER VIRTUE: The Divine Endowment

*"Who can find a virtuous woman? For her price is far above rubies.*

*The heart of her husband doth safely trust in her, so that he shall have no need of spoil.*

*A virtuous woman is a crown to her husband: but she that maketh ashamed is as rottenness in his bones.*

*For a man indeed ought not to cover his head, forasmuch, as he is the image and glory of God: but the woman is the glory of the man.*

*For the man is not of the woman; but the woman of the man.*

*Neither was the man created for the woman; but the woman for the man.*

*And the whole multitude sought to touch him: for there went virtue out of him, and healed them all."*

    **PROV. 31:10,11; 12:4; 1 COR. 11:7-9; LUKE 6:19.**

*"Who can find a virtuous woman? For her price is far above rubies"* **PROV. 31:10.**

If I may paraphrase this unique verse it will go like this 'Can anyone discover a woman of virtue? For her price is not negotiable! This expresses more the conception and delivery of this chapter on the woman's virtue as the Divine endowment that powers her price. What really is virtue and what is its source? Does every woman have the endowment of virtue or is it an elite reserve for the high and mighty and the rich and famous of women? If this is not then can a woman, any woman, be void or empty of virtue?

The Hebrew word for virtue **'Chayil'** means strength of mind or body. The woman's beauty is generated by the inner source of strength, empowered by her character and submission, even the ornament of a meek and quiet spirit which is in the sight of God of great price and the relativity is the beauty of God's holiness (Psa. 110:3; 1 Pet. 3:4).

Her virtue, however, is the empowerment of her price, the internal registration of power that produces external indications and creates an impact on the outside. God is the source of her virtue and the relativity is the power of God's holiness. The beauty of God's holiness generates character and submission in the woman, which gives her strength and beauty, while the power of God's holiness creates virtue, which gives her a price and the power to make an impact in her world.

*"A virtuous woman is a crown to her husband: but she that maketh ashamed is as rottenness in his bones"* **PROV. 12:4.**

A virtuous woman, not a girl but woman, is highlighted here as a crown. A crown connotes royalty and authority and depicts kingship. The man in the creation was made in the likeness and image of God, the king of the universe. Man was enthroned king on this side of the great divide and the woman God made to be positioned on the adjacent throne.

There is no king without a subject **neither** is there a king without a kingmaker. God, in His wisdom and purpose by design, has empowered the woman as both a subject and a kingmaker to the man. Her beauty in character and submission makes her a subject while her virtue, the Divine endowment of power, creates the impact that coronates the man as king.

'A virtuous woman is a crown to her husband' means she is married to a man not a concubine, girlfriend, lover or mistress. It takes a man to give definition to a woman. All she is and was created to be centers on a man. A woman's purpose must have a definition and the man is equipped to give that definition: **a crown;** the king is her husband and the coronation is the kingship of her husband in the permanence of marriage (PSALMS 45:13-16). The fruit of this relationship will produce princes and princesses that carry royalty and the capacity to maintain and propagate it on earth to the glory and praise of God.

*"And their seed shall be known among the Gentiles, and their offspring among people: all that see them shall acknowledge them, that they are the seed which the LORD hath blessed.*
*Her children arise up, and call her blessed; her husband also, and he praiseth her.* **ISAIAH 61:9; PROV. 31:28**

The seed of the woman and productivity of their godly relationship is highlighted here, connoting the sacredness of marriage and the power of virtue in the woman. God does not delight in the violation of women that leads to illegitimate birth of children and dissipation of her purpose. Unable to relate purpose to the man, her **shame** becomes **as the rottenness in his bones (PROV. 12:4).**

*"For a man indeed ought not to cover his head, for as much as he is the image and glory of God: but the woman is the glory of the man. For the man is not of the woman; but the woman of the man. Neither was the man created for the woman; but the woman for the man."*
**1 COR. 11:7-9.**

The Apostle Paul was highlighting here the role and conduct of the man and woman in fulfillment of God's purpose by design.

Solomon, in Proverbs, had already given us perspective that the virtuous woman is a crown to her husband and a crowned man need not cover his head other than with his crown which symbolizes kingship and royalty; for he is the image and glory of God, the Most High King. **God is the ONLY one who can break a man down without crushing his spirit** and He does this most times through the **virtue** of the woman. By mystery of divine endowment and relativity, God empowers the woman to break the man down from excesses that makes him a dictator to a king that rules with justice and mercy through the woman's power of submission; not a passive allegiance but an active rest and trust.

*"The heart of her husband doth safely trust in her, so that he will have no need of spoil.*
*She will do him good and not evil all the days of her life.*
*Her husband is known in the gates, when he sitteth among the elders of the land."*
**PROV. 31:11,12,23.**

The man's world cannot hold without the woman's presence and essence of virtue. The Divine purpose by design gives her a place, a pivot role, consequential to the coronation of the man and establishment of his domain. When she is relegated or downtrodden, the man suffers damage to his mission and when she fails to submit and surrender in **trust,** she is displaced and falls out of orbit of God's fulfillment of her. Either way it works to her detriment or to the man's **dysfunction.**

My father in the LORD, Dr. Emmanuel Folarin, gave me an insight through his inspired teaching ministry when he taught about the five-letter word of the woman and described them as components of her virtue. The **WOMAN** is described as a Winner-Organizer-Manager-Administrator-Neutralizer / Nourisher, and this makes her a woman, a virtuous woman.

**As a Winner,** she wins the heart of her husband.
*"The heart of her husband doth safely trust in her, so that he shall have no need of spoil."* **PROV. 31:11.**
**Spoil** is the reward for warriors after a victorious battle. The woman becomes the prize of the man's conquest and prowess, his choice possession, and in her he finds a pearl of great price, both

a fixed and liquid asset. She becomes the door and gateway to his heart and life.

**As an Organizer,** she is fitted with passion, the spring of inspiration that builds the man and makes him a home.

*"She seeketh wool, and flax and worketh willingly with her hands.*
*She considereth a field, and buyeth it: with the fruit of her hands she planteth a vineyard.*
*She girdeth her lions with strength, and strengtheneth her arms."*

**PROV. 31:13,16,17.**

Her role as an organizer brings out most her beauty and the strength of her character. Her passion creates energy, enthusiasm and strength, creating an impact that spurs the man to excellence and lofty heights. The dexterous hands weaving intricate details of love and purpose into the fabric of a man's life, giving meaning and bringing comfort. With his resources the man builds a shelter, a nest of protection, but the woman alone is inspired to organize the climate of comfort and make it a place called home. With a virtue that can only be termed as Divine endowment, she organizes a home where the man is treated as king with courtesy, submission and compassion that fails to be accorded him at work; holding distractions at bay and streamlining his focus to objectivity and creativity. She is girded with the strength of character and submission, shod with the shoes of iron and brass, which gives her lasting beauty.

(Deut. 33:25).

**As a Manager,** she is equipped with the dynamics of Home Economics and Resource Management. She oversees and manages the resources the man provides, utilizing them for maximum result.

*"She layeth her hands to the spindle, and her hands hold the distaff. She strecheth out her hands to the poor: yea, she reacheth forth her hands to the needy.*
*She is not afraid of the snow for her household: for all her household are clothed with scarlet.*

*She maketh her coverings of tapestry: her clothing is silk and purple. She maketh fine linen, and selleth it: and delivereth girdles unto the merchant.*

**PROV. 31:19-22,24.**

She is the perfect supplement to the man, needed to complement his function. She is the treasure reserve of her man. She also carries the trademark of compassion: giving, and like Christ, her virtue carries the power to affect the poor and needy around her with the touch of love (Luke 6:19). Not afraid of the prospect of scarcity, figuratively the snow of winter, she has her family covered with her reserve.

**As an Administrator,** she is the minister of love and healing, peace and harmony in the home. Without wisdom, the home becomes a house with a king who operates with a dictator style divide and rule policy. It takes wisdom to bring equilibrium to man's world and peace to the home where the heat is greatest and the temperature highest.

*"EVERY wise woman buildeth her house: but the foolish plucketh it down with her hands.*

*Through wisdom is a house builded; and by understanding it is established.*

*She openeth her mouth with wisdom, and in her tongue is the law of kindness.*

*She looketh well to the ways of her household, and eateth not the bread of idleness."*

**PROV. 14:1; 24:3; 31:26,17.**

She is endowed with divine wisdom to work for the productive benefit of the man and home. The man needs a place called home and the woman creates the atmosphere called home. With a tongue **coated** with the law of kindness, she breaks the man's excesses and builds him up to be God's man.

**As a Neutralizer and Nourisher,** she acts as a circuit breaker to the man. Tension and stress is generated by the competition in the man's world, the demand of his work and the interchange of ideas and interaction with his environment. The woman comes in to neutralize tension, kill stress and reduce distractions. She nourishes his body with food and tantalizes his senses with the delights of her body.

With man's body and soul needs fully covered, man can face his work rest assured that it will be well worth the effort with the availability of a nourisher and perfect tranquilizer in his wife to diffuse his tension, streamline his focus and keep him going.

*"She is like the merchant's ships; she bringeth her food from afar.*
*She riseth also while it is yet night, and giveth meat to her husband, and a portion to her maidens.*
*Her husband is known in the gates, when he siteth among the elders of the land. Her children arise up, and call her blessed; her husband also, and he praiseth her."*

**PROV. 31:14-15,23,28.**

She provides both edible food for her household and the provender of sex to her man. She nourishes her husband with delights, breaking rigidity and resistance, flexing mind and muscle. She nurtures the man's wounded spirit and bruised ego to revive his fighting spirit and conquering prowess. Healed and restored, he goes on to conquer his world and become known in the land as a winner.

**Her children sing her praise and her husband join the refrain.**

God, in all, is praised in glory!

The virtuous woman is a complete woman, God's woman with a price and her price is not negotiable. She is all that is needed to make a man's world hold and take form.

*"She girdeth her loins with strength, and strengtheneth her arms.*
*She perceiveth that her merchandise is good: her candle goeth not out by night. Strength and honor are her clothing; and she shall rejoice in time to come."*

**PROV. 31:17-18,25.**

She builds up her armory with the ornament of a meek and quiet spirit (1 Pet. 3:4). No one wins a battle by manufacturing weapons on the battlefield. She knows her worth and the capacity of her essence, her effect and impact on the man and she does not experience burnout. She is not a superwoman or bionic in strength, she is made of like passion in flesh and blood and subject to the limitations and frustration of the fall. However, she is endowed with virtue, God's empowerment, and restored to purpose through submission to God's way of life and precept for fulfillment.

Today's woman is a burned out wreak, far from purpose and afflicted with fear and insecurity owing to sin and deflection. When we drift from the truth of God's purpose by design it becomes a wide tangent and the farther you go the wider the tangent. But the puzzle becomes solved by the revelation and definition of the Maker of mankind. Restoration is found only in God's word, God's instruction manual for fulfillment.

I came across a story about the Mayor of a US city and his wife.

The couple drove down to a gas station to obtain gas and while there, the woman noticed that the gas attendant was familiar. The man happened to be a former boyfriend and old memories came rushing. They exchanged pleasantries, talked and later parted. While in the car, the Mayor quizzed his wife, having noticed she was excited about the gasman, and asked if she was not excited being married to a Mayor while her former lover is only a gas attendant.

To this she replied that if she had married the gasman he would have turned out to be the Mayor, while he, the Mayor, would have been the gasman. This woman understood the power of a woman's virtue. She knew her worth, her impact and effect in a man's life **and world,** and she understood her price.

At the fall, a depletion of divine virtue occurred, leading to the loss of strength and honor in the woman.

*"A virtuous woman is a crown to her husband: but she that maketh ashamed is as rottenness in his bones.*
*Strength and honour are her clothing; and she shall rejoice in time to come."*
**PROV. 12:4; 31:25.**

In the garden, the man and the woman were naked and were not ashamed (Gen. 2:25). The first awareness, however, that struck them after eating the fruit in disobedience was that of their nakedness.

Satanic awareness filled them with shame as they became stripped of the glory of God that covered them (Gen. 3:7-13).

The man lost the glory and authority of God in him, the key to his dominion and productivity in his mission, the divine assignment for his life. The woman lost the relativity of God's essence endowed on her, chiefly her virtue, and the power to crown her husband king, which was the key to her fulfillment. While the deflection brought shame on their relationship and wreaked havoc to their purpose, she became to Adam **as the rottenness in his bones** (Prov. 12:4).

'And Adam was not deceived, but the woman being deceived was in the transgression'

(1 Tim. 2:14). The satanic negotiation took its toll on the woman as that rottenness reproduced itself in the daughters born to man of the woman, and that abscess has brought deflection to the destinies of men throughout the ages (Gen. 6:1-5). The carnage and depletion of divine substance and essence relevant to complement the man's role in fulfilling his God-given task of dominating and replenishing the earth. She has been relegated, dislocated and displaced out of orbit; mentally disrobed of her honour and dignity and spiritually disvirgined of her destiny and eternal relevance.

Her essence and presence reflects the eternal virtue and character of God the Almighty. Beyond the cosmetic appeal of her body and the domestic appraisal of her role, lies a grand purpose by design of her Maker. This translates her relativity and relevance into eternal dimensions. Beyond the domestic monument of the home, is God showing His everlasting beauty and enduring mercy through the essence and character of the woman.

The debacle stripped the woman of her clothing of **strength and honor** and killed the prospect of a joyful future (Prov. 31:25).

Reduced to ground zero, the man became uncrowned; a king without a subject, void of authority in his own domain while his queen, meant to occupy the adjacent throne, became **as rottenness in his bones.** Virtue is all the woman needed to set her in orbit and keep God's Milky Way of purpose by design working. She was created and empowered to crown man and produce his subjects. Her purpose made her unique and her price was far above rubies, not negotiable.

Her shameful fall, however, brought violation to man's royalty, deflection to his purpose and focus, corruption to his subjects (his seed and the creation inclusive) and negotiation to her price. The conclusion is sobering and the implications far reaching; violation epidemics of enormous and frightening proportions created by sin, the satanic nature in mankind.

The fog of spiritual darkness permeated the world suffocating souls and creating pandemic deflection and manipulation until the light of God, in Jesus the sun of righteousness and the bright and morning star, shone brilliantly through, dispelling the darkness.

(Mal. 4:2; Rev. 22:16).

*"In him was life; and the life was the light of men.*
*And the light shineth in darkness; and the darkness comprehended it not.*
*That was the true light, which lighteth every man that cometh into the world."*

**JOHN 1:4-5,8**

Before anything could be done God had to light up the world, pushing back the darkness.

He lighted up the world with Jesus, the Word made flesh, forcing the darkness to a retreat.

This light was deposited in every one that was born into the world, making us stars destined to shine in God's orbit and reflecting His glory (1Cor. 15:41). Sin created a deflection of that light in us at birth through the negotiation pact, turning the light inwards, that we became burned out stars, black holes in burned out space, reserved for the blackness of darkness forever.

**JUDE 1:13.**

*"For God who commanded the light to shine out of darkness, hath shined in our hearts, to give the light of the knowledge of the glory of God in the face of Jesus Christ.*
*Who hath delivered us from the power of darkness, and hath translated us into the kingdom of his dear son.*

**11 COR. 4:6; COL. 1:13.**

Jesus brought the light of God into our world to dispel the darkness and restore purpose. The restoration of mankind was effected through the cross of Jesus and the blood of His redemption.

Redemption is available to all, one life at a time, but everyone must come to Jesus in faith and trust to be restored to the glory of God. Jesus is the Bright and Morning Star and without Him our world remains eternally dark, our purpose defeated, our focus deflected and our lives doomed for eternal darkness.

As many as would believe, Jesus restores the true purpose for our creation, the key to our fulfillment, and gives us the light to guide us through.

*"For ye were sometimes darkness, but now are ye light in the world: walk as children of light; that ye should shew forth the praises of him who hath called you out of darkness into his marvelous light; as unto a light that shineth in a dark place, until the day down, and the daystar arise in your hearts."*

**EPH. 5:8; 1 PET. 2:9; 11 PET. 1:19.**

We are charged with the mandate to remain and walk in the light to keep the deflection of darkness at bay, and only in walking in the light can we receive the divine nature and fulfill our purpose for creation (Phil. 4:8; 11 Pet. 1:3-8).

*"AND THE WHOLE MULTITUDE SOUGHT TO TOUCH HIM: FOR THERE WENT VIRTUE OUT OF HIM, AND HEALED THEM ALL."* **LUKE 6:19.**

Jesus brought virtue, God's power of redemption, restoration and completion, back to our world. He came to set the captives free and to restore purpose and power by His blood. The woman, God's woman, can be restored to the glorious purpose of Divine virtue endowed on her again. Virtue to bring wholeness and healing to the sin-deformed souls of as many as would touch Him in faith.

*"And Jesus said somebody hath touched me: for I perceive that virtue is gone out of me."*

**LUKE 8:46.**

A woman reached out in simple faith and simply touched the garment of Jesus. What made the difference, however, was the impact received from that touch-it healed her flow of blood.

Virtue brought wholeness to her sin-deformed soul as she touched Him in faith. The satanic negotiation on her life, the carnage, the depletion of divine substance and essence relevant to create her world and place her in orbit, the violation of her purpose, was stopped by the power of Jesus. She became restored and made whole as virtue came out of Jesus and is still out today. Out to restore the woman to God's orbit of grace and fulfillment and make her a crown to her husband, endowed with divine virtue.

Out to restore man to dominion and authority. Out to stop the satanic violation and negotiation in the woman, end the carnage and depletion, and restore her price. Through the blood, God's negotiable instrument, she is fully restored. At the cross of Calvary, Jesus gave His virtue a permanent outing to enforce a final stopping of the enemy. Reach out, touch it and be made whole for **virtue is gone out of me,** *saith* the LORD!

A woman's virtue is displayed in her purity and virginity, which bonds her to one man and once for life, ensuring the beauty of permanence and the proper nourishing of her man in marriage.

It is released in her Love, the unconditional choice that makes her stick to her man for life. It is revealed in her passion, the spring of inspiration and creative skill, which propels her to build up the man and make him a home.

It shines through her Beauty, the inner strength of character and submission, which brings her fulfillment and the productivity of the family. It governs through the Home Economic Dynamics of her virtue, which crowns the husband and creates equilibrium in his life and home.

Her virtue is sustained by **her growth: the power of appreciation.**

# HER GROWTH: The Power of Appreciation

*And God blessed them, and God said unto them, Be fruitful, and multiply, and replenish the earth, and subdue it: and have dominion over the fish of the sea, and over the fowl of the air, and over every living thing that moveth upon the earth.*

*And God saw everything that he had made, and, behold, it was very good. And the evening and the morning were the sixth day. And the LORD God took the man, and put him into the Garden of Eden to dress it and to keep it. And the rib, which the LORD God had taken from man, made he a woman, and brought her unto the man. And Adam said, this is now bone of my bones, and flesh of my flesh: she shall be called Woman, because she was taken out of man.*

*And Adam called his wife's name Eve; because she was the mother of all living. To every thing there is a season, and a time to every purpose under the heaven. He hath made every thing beautiful in His time: also he hath set the world in their heart, so that no man can find out the work that God maketh from the beginning to the end.*

*Except a corn of wheat fall into the ground and die, it abideth alone: but if it die, it bringeth forth much fruit. Because the creature itself also shall be delivered from the bondage of corruption into the glorious liberty of the children of God and they that use this world, as not abusing it: for the fashion of this world passeth away.*

*Likewise, ye husbands dwell with them according to knowledge, giving honour unto the wife, as unto the weaker vessel, and as being heirs together of the grace of life; that your prayers be not hindered.* **GEN. 1:28, 31; 2:15, 22, 23; 3:20; ECC. 3:1, 11; JOHN 12:24; ROM. 8:21; I COR. 7:31; 1 PETER 3:7.**

*"And God blessed them, and God said unto them, Be fruitful, and multiply, and replenish the earth, and subdue it: and have dominion over the fish of the sea, and over the fowl of the air, and over every living thing that moveth upon the earth"*

The first charge and blessing God gave man after the creation was put in place was to be fruitful, and multiply, and replenish the earth (Gen 1:28). The divine attribute of perfection and authority endowed on man empowered him to be fruitful and to multiply, subdue, and have dominion over all creatures in the earth. The clause, however, was the replenishing of the earth, which had to do with the character and attitude of man towards the creation. This was well before Eve was formed. The replenishing process is all about appraisal and appreciation. We cannot appreciate that which we have not apprised. Appraisal brings value to the creation, which leads to appreciation and replenishing of the earth. The power of imagination cannot be as strong as the power of appreciation. You appreciate and get inspired by what you see but what you imagine is not real.

Adam's mental prowess was proved by the power of imagination. His field of vision, however, inspired him to worship. God had dotted the landscape with wildlife and trees **'that are pleasant to the sight' (Gen. 2:9)** for man's pleasure and food. God then brought all creatures He made for Adam to **'see'** and **'name'** (Gen. 2:19) and his appraisal became God's approval. The phrase **'and God saw that it was good'** appears seven times in the story of creation in Genesis 1, after which God certified creation **'very good'** at the end (Gen. 1:31).

By constant appraisal of the creation, Adam came to appreciate and worship the Maker of it all. That appreciation brought growth to his relationship with God. Replenishing the earth meant to accord names to each creature, defining their habitat and other intricacies of their existence, and caring for them with an attitude and character that depicted the mind of the Creator
(Psalms 145:9, 13, 16-17).

*"Thy righteousness is like the great mountains; thy judgments are a great deep: O LORD, thou preservest man and beast."*

**PSALM 36:6**

In celebrating the wonder of God's creation, man was to replenish the earth by appreciating and caring for all that He has made. The charge to replenish the earth placed man as a **"keeper and dresser"** of God's garden, Eden (Gen. 2:15; Ezek 28:13).

For *'the earth is the LORD's, and the fullness therefore; the world, and they that dwell therein'* (Psalm 24:1). Everything God made caries the signature of God. They are so constructed as to show the most consummate wisdom in their design, and in the end for which they are formed. They are all God's property, and should be used only in reference to the end for which they were created.

All creation bears the force of life and carries the capacity to grow, relatively or absolutely. Growth is a sign of life and the force of growth is the power of appreciation endowed on man, which ensures the replenishing of the earth, through cultivation and care of the creation.

God instilled life into man, the animals, the plants, and the lifeless but dynamic forces of the earth, crowning creation with compassion and care. He notes even the death of a common sparrow when it falls to the ground. While the sermon on the mount expressly states that God values man above the creatures (Matt. 6:25-34), the entire thrust of scripture – from paradise lost in Genesis to paradise regained in Revelation – is that God treasures and takes pleasure not in man alone but in everything He created: ***"For thou hast created all things, and for thy pleasure they are and were created."*** (Rev. 4:11).

**'Because the creature itself also shall be delivered from the bondage of corruption into the glorious liberty of the children of God'** (Rom. 8:21). God cares for the creation in relativity to the way that a mother cares for the one she has given birth to.

Man was charged to develop an administration of tenderness toward all creatures made subject to him and a care that do not lessen the sweetness of life in the animal creation which the great

Creator intends for them under our administration. This was the only medium by which the replenishing process could be maintained.

Adam was mandated to dress the Garden, to keep it in a state of appreciation, to ensure that the beauty and grandeur God has reflected in nature is not despoiled. We care for the animals not because whales are our brothers, but because animals are part of God's kingdom over which we are to exercise dominion. Appreciation is all about celebrating the wonder of God in creation and this comes by taking every opportunity to demonstrate to the watching world a proper concern and care for all things that comes from the hand of our Creator.

Adam was made a great pulpiteer in the sanctuary of creation to lead the creatures' praise to God the Maker. And we all join in appreciation by recognising and enjoying our humble position as fellow worshipers with a natural world, mysteriously blending together to give praise to our mutual Creator, Sustainer, and Redeemer.

From the divine dimension, the creation is being appraised and replenished by the maintenance of seedtime and harvest, cold and heat, summer and winter, and day and right (Gen. 8:22).

From man's angle, by acknowledging God's care and concern for the entire creation and seeking to do all we can to demonstrate and extend that care – especially by refraining from abusing what He loves and cares for.

*"For the invisible things of Him from the creation of the world are clearly seen, being understood by the things that are made, even his eternal power and God head; so that they are without excuse'*

**ROMANS 1:20.**

Ignorance is no excuse for the abuse of God's creation as God holds man accountable for all violations against the creation. In Psalm 19, David reminds us that God speaks to us through two books. One is the written word of God (Psalm 19:7-11). The other revelation is the masterpiece of creation, which eloquently reveals God to every person everyday. God has created all people in all times from the very beginning with such an awareness, and it echoes in one loud refrain, *'Replenish the earth'* (Gen. 1:28). This was the same charge God gave Noah after the flood.

**"And God blessed Noah and his sons, and said unto them, Be fruitful, and multiply, and replenish the earth". GEN. 9:1.**

Life must go on, and purpose must be achieved, but this could only be by replenishing or appraising the earth through cultivation and care. Everything appreciated grows, in value or in substance. When creation is appreciated, it leads to replenishing that causes the earth to produce and bring forth fruit. We cannot survive without the fruit of the earth. We are totally dependent upon the fruitfulness of the creation for our health and livelihood (Psalms 104:14-15, 27-30).

Growth is all about time and it comes with the appreciation of time.

*"To every thing there is a season, and a time to every purpose under the heaven.*
*He hath made everything beautiful in his time: also he hath set the world in their heart, so that no man can find out the work that God maketh from the beginning to the end."*
**ECCLESIASTES 3:1, 11**

In the course of time, God made the woman and brought her to Adam, empowered with mental perfection. Adam was able to encapsulate God's mercy and love for him into a five star word 'WOMAN'; the very name God purposed and which was a key to her function. She was a blend of purpose by design, a divine masterpiece and a force of relatively to man.

The name, woman, means bone of my bones and flesh of my flesh, one with me, which denotes equality and balance. In essence he was saying that they were made of the same substance and material. Balance is only possible between two equals. Balance is the signature of God. God made man of the dust of the earth, crude and absolute, and from the crude material of the man God formed a woman. A refined product of crude dust she became. God then brought her unto Adam to produce equilibrium and a perfect blend, the crude complementing the refined.

***We were born for connection.*** We are designed to fill a need. Relatively or absolutely we become the solution to another person's problem. The sun was designed to rule by day and the moon was to rule the night. Both complement each other to fulfil a 24-hour day timeframe. The moon can actually do what the sun can never do – **shine at night.**

It was God Himself who shut the womb of Hannah to meet a need, relatively and absolutely

(1 Sam. 1:5). She needed a son and God needed a prophet, the blending of both need created a miracle: a son, relative to her need and, a prophet, absolutely to God's need (1Sam. 1:26-28).

The God who created Nineveh also created Jonah. God is the righteous judge and in His eternal love and justice He ensures that no faithful man or woman lose out both ways. He gives everyone a chance. God compensates me for what you have and I don't and compensate you for what I have and you don't. Your sufficiency fills my deficiency and vice versa. God then expects us to complement each other. Jesus explained in scripture:

*"Thou shall love the Lord thy God with all thy heart, and with all thy soul, and with all thy mind. This is the first and great commandment. And the second is like unto it, thou shall love thy neighbour as thyself." **MATTHEW 22:37 – 39.***

The cross is simply a vertical relationship of man's dependence on God and a horizontal relationship of our dependence on each other. First we are a product of God's love and grace, then, a product of His help and goodwill through fellow men.

Jesus again taught, 'Blessed are they which do hunger and thirst… for they shall be filled

(Matt. 5:6). God creates the thirst to fill in the need for *'two are better than one; because they have a good reward for their labour'* (Ecc. 4:9).

The woman became God's higher Garden made in fleshly proportions. As highlighted in previous chapters, her body, the force of relativity, was a typical garden for man. This comprised her nakedness, the exposed or bare garden, which formed the beauty of suspense to man and gave him mental pleasure like the beautiful landscape of the literal garden.

Her virginity formed the gate to the tree of life, the reserved part of the garden, while her sexuality was the fountain of nourishment, the life-giving stream. Her love was the unconditional assurance to man that she will always be there for him and her passion was the inspiration needed to build man and make him a home, an environment of comfort and healing where the making of his dream is achieved.

Her beauty came from the inner source, giving her the strength of character and submission, which made her a subject and her virtue, the divine endowment, empowered her to make man king and made her a crown to the man.

The divine essence endowed on the woman and contained in her body, the force of relativity to man, bore the force of life and carried the capacity of growth, relatively and absolutely.

Just as man was mandated to dress the Garden and keep it, man was equally charged to

*'Be fruitful, and multiply, and replenish the earth, and subdue it'*
empowered by God's blessing on man (Gen. 1:28).

The woman, however, creates the environment where this charge is fulfilled and it is only maintained by her growth, which comes by the power of appreciation endowed on man. Divine love, Agape, is the power of appreciation and the force of growth.

That love, called Agape, is invested in the heart of the man, not the woman. That love is defined in scripture and it is a reference to God; no other place can it be found.

The woman is the object, the relativity, of that love but it takes the man to work or call out that love in appreciation and give it a definition. In like manner, people are the object of God's love, relatively and absolutely, but it took Christ Jesus to work out that love in us and give it a definition: **the church** (Eph. 5:25). Agape is the love that is called out of the heart of the lover as a result of the value he has placed on the object of his love. In this light, therefore, love is the power of appreciation that gives value and creates growth and replenishing both in the earth and in the woman. Adam was mandated to give names to all creatures, define their habitat and care for them, giving value to the creation, which brought replenishing to the earth. He equally named his help meet 'woman', giving definition to her function **'womanhood'** and was empowered to bring fulfilment to her in the habitat of marriage.

Her growth and replenishing would be sustained by love, the power of appreciation, owing to her value and placed on her by man. The replenishing process is all about appraisal and appreciation. We cannot appreciate that which we have not apprised. Appraisal brings value to the creation, which leads to appreciation and replenishing of the earth.

A king is strengthened by the growth and stability of his kingdom. A woman, however, is replenished by the power of appreciation, the love and value invested on her by her man, which causes her to grow, relatively and absolutely, as her seed is multiplied in the earth and God is glorified on high. Adam was charged to dress the Garden, to keep it in a state of appreciation, and to ensure that the beauty and grandeur God has revealed in nature is not violated or abused. We are thus charged, *"And they that use this world, as not abusing it* (1COR. 7:31).

He was given a love for God that affected the creatures of the earth, which formed his domain. And only by appreciating and demonstrating a proper concern for all things that comes from the hand of the Creator could the earth be replenished and subdued.

However, God made a better neighbour for him to love as himself: **the woman** whom he named Woman, defined her habitat: marriage, and other intricacies of her existence: **bone of my bones, flesh of my flesh, one with me, my helper.**

And he was to care for her with an attitude and character that depicted the mind of God, the Creator, in relativity to other creatures. Their marriage would then bring about the replenishing and subduing of the earth.

Marriage is from beginning to the end a divine phenomenon. Marriage begins and ends with God. Marriage can only attain God's frequency of purpose by design when it carries the signature of God, which is equilibrium and order. When man appreciates and aligns to the order of God in creation there is bound to be growth and replenishing in the earth and when this dimension of replenishing sets in the family, the woman will grow to become a stalwart of virtue and strength through the power of appreciation.

*"How long wilt thou go about, O thou backsliding daughter? For the LORD hath created a new thing upon the earth, A woman shall compass a man."*

**JEREMIAH 31:22.**

The word '**compass**' is the Hebrew word '**cabab**' pronounced '**shawbab**', and it means "to revolve, to surround, to form a border around, to besiege, to create an environment around."

This tells us that a wife is empowered by God to create an environment around the husband. Her endowment of the divine essence of love, passion, beauty and virtue empowers her to protect the man's focus, reduce distraction thereby streamlining him to excellence in his assignment, and creating the environment where his dreams are hatched and bud in fruition. This gives her a price and her price is not negotiable.

A beautiful Garden surrounded Adam but he had to keep it and dress it, to keep it in a state of appreciation, for maximum productivity and the replenishing of the earth. Relatively, the woman's body, with its delicate design and structure, has to be dressed and kept in a state of appreciation, in essence and presence, for maximum productivity in nourishment and the replenishing of the earth in procreation.

So many people come short in just admiring others. Admiration is intellectual and borders on the sight of the eyes and the working of the brain. Appreciation, however, goes beyond the veil to call out the hidden goodness, the best in people to surface.

You can go on to appreciate others even if they do not appeal by their looks. Appreciation is of the heart and therefore spiritual. It is based on the unconditional love of God deposited in us and it looks on the image of God in people, not their deformed character or bodies. It accepts unconditionally without cost or error, not considering flaws and inadequacies.

Little wonder, when people are not appreciated by an insensitive world they become deformed in character and begin to wither in the scorching heat of hostility while depreciation sets in. Only those who have the power of appreciation can turn darkness into light, give beauty for ashes, hope for despair and become relevant in a cold and cynical world. Appreciation calls out the best in people and situations and ultimately leads to the replenishing of the earth.

If a man will invest into his wife unconditional love and value, the power of appreciation, 'a woman shall, indeed, compass a man". In the midst of darkness she will be your light and in the midst of sorrow she will be your joy. When there is a casting down, she will be your lifting up. When the tides are high and your despair draws nigh, she will be your equilibrium and balance to make you stay. *"And they that use this world, as not abusing it: for the fashion of this world passeth away."* **1 COR. 7:31**.

The first form of abuse came about in marriage when man failed to protect the woman and exposed her to the serpent's temptation while being there "WITH HER" in the Garden
(Gen. 3:6). This brought corruption to her body (as well as the Garden), dissipated her purpose, and led to the violation and pollution we find in the earth today generally called **'abuse'**. The relationship between husbands and wives was strategically placed in scripture before the caution on world abuse was given (1 COR. 7:29 – 31).

Failure to appraise the role and appreciate the value of the woman eventually leads to abuse and depletion of divine substance both in the material creation and the domestic monument of the home and marriage.

These includes human – caused global climate change, air and water pollution, soil erosion, noise pollution, species loss, and fisheries depletion which comprise the world of man's literal Garden. On the other hand, the relative garden of the woman has been defiled, violated and abused culminating in sexual abuse, social dislocation and relegation, mental disrobing of her honour and dignity. This has lead to moral decay, pandemic anarchy, dysfunctional families and societies and a generation steeped in addictions beyond conviction; victimised children, lost youth, sexual pervasion that goes unchallenged. The general warfare against children as the onslaught of abortion is heralded in the vanguard of modern life; children abandoned, abused, drugged, bombed, neglected, poorly raised, poorly fed, poorly taught, and poorly disciplined. Born into an abused, depleted, diseased, and poisoned world.

The earth reeling under the abuse of mankind **'groaneth and travaileth in pain together until now'** (Rom. 8:22).

It was in this setting that Jesus, the seed of the woman, was born to redeem man from the curse and stop the abuse in the world of man. Jesus said in scripture.

*"Verily, verily, I say unto you, except a corn of wheat fall into the ground and die, it abideth alone: but if it die, it bringeth forth much fruit".* **JOHN 12:24.**

The replenishing process of growth also requires death and resurrection. **'Seedtime and harvest'** can be interpreted as death and resurrection. ***"So also is the resurrection of the dead. It is sown in corruption, it is raised in incorruption; it is sown in dishonour; it is raised in glory: it is sown in weakness; it is raised in power"*** (1 COR. 15:42 – 43).

Except a corn of wheat fall into the ground and die, it abides alone. How relative or absolute is this truth of scripture? In Genesis 2:22, 23, Adam identified his helpmeet and called her 'woman'. Woman means bone of my bones, and flesh of my flesh. The name spelt her oneness and equality with him, her function and purpose, and gave her an identity.

However, in Genesis 3 a clause was introduced as the woman **'died'** a spiritual death through sin but this led to the circumstances that made her multiply and replenish the earth through childbirth. In Genesis 3:20, Adam again spelt this function by naming her '**Eve**' meaning 'life giver or mother of the living, different from the first name, woman, which means equal.

*"And Adam called his wife's name Eve; because she has the mother of all living".*

Genesis 4:1 presented the function of Eve as she conceived and brought forth her first child. In appreciation, her growth multiplied and replenished the earth with the seed of Adam. Propagating and reproducing until the seed of the woman, Jesus Christ, came through

Virgin Mary. Growing up *'as a tender plant, and as a root out of a dry ground; He was despised and rejected of men; a man of sorrows, and acquainted with grief as the LORD laid on Him the iniquity of us all* (ISA. 53:2-6). He became as 'a corn of wheat that fell into the ground and died' as 'he was cut off out of the land of the living' (ISA. 53:8). He was sown in the body of corruption but raised in the glory of incorruption' (1 COR. 15:42).

Triumphantly, His death and resurrection led to the replenishing of God's restored earth; 'For it became Him, for whom are all things, and by whom are all things, in bringing many sons unto glory, to make the captain of their salvation perfect through sufferings' (Heb. 2:10). He shall see the travail of his soul, and shall be satisfied: by His knowledge shall my righteous servant justify many; for he shall bear their iniquities. For whom He did foreknow; he also did predestinate to be conformed to the image of his son, that He might be the firstborn among many brethren. (ISA. 53:11; ROM. 8:29).

*"And He is the head of the body, the church; who is the beginning, the firstborn from the dead; that in all things He might have the pre-eminence. And from Jesus Christ, who is the faithful witness, and the first begotten of the dead, and the Prince of the kings of the earth. Unto Him that loved us, and washed us from our sins in His own blood. And hath made us kings and priest unto God and His Father; to Him be glory and dominion for ever and ever, Amen"* **COL. 1:18; REV. 1:5-6.**

God's conclusion of His creation in Genesis was that it was very good, good in every situation, even when rebellion brought sin and corruption to creation, God foresaw and spoke restoration through the seed of the woman. Though *'the eyes of the LORD are in every place, beholding the evil and the good'* yet *'God commended His love toward us, in that, while we were yet sinners, Christ died for us'* (PROV. 15:3; Rom. 5:8). For by His grace we are saved and of His fullness have all we received, even grace for grace (Eph. 2:9; John 1:16). God's appreciation of His creation in us and the appraisal of His salvation cause us to grow in His grace, even in a hostile world ruled by Satan, *'not imputing their trespasses unto them'* (2 COR. 5:19; EPH. 2:19-22; 2 PET. 3:18).

Due to the congenital defect in us, owing to the fall, and the infirmities of sin that constantly beset us, God is not holding us to ransom or forcing a verdict of allegiance on us but He supplies more grace as we humble ourselves before Him.

*"But where sin abounded, grace did much more abound: that as sin hath reigned unto death, even so might grace reign through righteousness unto eternal life by Jesus Christ our Lord;"* **ROM. 5:20, 21.**

All we need to grow is the supply of the grace of the Almighty, who loved us and washed us in His own blood. His appreciation and unconditional value of love placed on us supplies that grace to us *'who are kept by the power of God through faith'* (1 Peter 1:5).

Our growth is predicated on the appreciation of His grace in our lives. There is power in appreciation; power in appraisal and unconditional love and value that brings out the good from ugliness, call light out of darkness, give beauty for ashes, hope for despair and restore life to the dead. Appreciation brings a manifold cure in the growth of the woman and to the replenishing of the earth: *'Because the creature itself also shall be delivered from the bondage of corruption into the glorious liberty of the children of God'* (Rom. 8:21).

*"Likewise, ye husbands, dwell with them according to knowledge, giving honour unto the wife, as unto the weaker vessels, and as being heirs together of the grace of life; that your prayers be not hindered."* **1 PETER 3:7.**

Just as Adam was mandated to dress the Garden, to keep it appreciating, the man is specifically charged to relate to the woman with understanding, attributing to her honour, as the weaker vessel. The grace of God brings us all to equilibrium and gives us capacity to overcome and fulfill our purpose according to design. The woman is delicate but her function cannot be overemphasized, **strength and honour are her clothing; and she shall rejoice in time to come'** (PROV. 31:25). For that reason, her role is not to be played down or relegated, neither is the man's role superior, the blend of roles creates equilibrium and produces order.

She will, over the years, grow to become a stalwart like the vine… *'Neither shall your vine cast her fruit before the time in the field, saith the LORD of hosts'* (Mal. 3:11).

The vine is a unique tree, tender and weak when planted, it grows to become a bulwark of strength and stability, producing fruit fit for consumption after a time biblically defined as 'five (5) years' (Leviticus 19:23 – 25).

The woman's growth comes in the process of time through the power of appreciation and value invested on her. The vine's biblically defined term of five years for growth is relative and the woman, literally, may take a longer time, or even a lifetime, to grow. With the constant input of appreciation and value, however, her growth and replenishing is sure to be.

God's grace empowers us to fulfil our purpose as we function according to God's design. The man creates her growth by the power of appreciation and appraisal of her role. This would work to produce the glory of God in the creation and would remove hindrances to our prayers. With her place recognized and glory restored, her growth appreciates as she multiplies the seed of man in an atmosphere of love and harmony. This in turn leads to the replenishing of the earth as man takes the lead of the creatures' praise in creation's cathedral.

With the woman's growth assured, **her past** is covered by **the grace of redemption.**

# HER PAST: The Grace of Redemption

*"And Adam was not deceived, but the woman being deceived was in the transgression.*
*And there appeared a great wonder in heaven; a woman clothed with the sun, and the moon under her feet, and upon her head a crown of twelve stars:*
*And she being with child cried, travailing in birth, and pained to be delivered.*
*And there appeared another wonder in heaven; and behold a great red dragon, having seven heads and ten horns, and seven crowns upon his heads.*
*And his tail drew the third part of the stars of heaven, and did cast them to the earth: and the dragon stood before the woman which was ready to be delivered, for to devour her child as soon as it was born.*
*And she brought forth a man-child, who was to rule all nations with a rod of iron; and her child was caught up unto God, and to his throne.*
*And when the dragon saw that he was cast unto the earth, he persecuted the woman, which brought forth the man-child. And the dragon was wroth with the woman, and went to make war with the remnant of her seed, which keep the commandments of God and have the testimony of Jesus Christ. And when Jesus saw her, he called her to him, and said unto her, woman, thou art loosed from thine infirmity"*

    1 TIM. 2:14; REV. 12:1-5, 13, 17; LUKE 13:12.

*And I find more bitter than death the woman, whose heart is snare and nets, and her hands as bands: whoso pleaseth God shall escape from her; but the sinner shall be taken by her"*.ECC. 7:26

What are the circumstances that led to this detail of a woman in the inspired collection of the Holy Writ? Was she defective in creation or was her past irredeemable?

What brought about such degradation, relegation and negation of her essence and relevance? The inspired word of God here portrays her as a caricature of the divine portrait and, surely, must be abhorred of God, as there is a provision of immunity from her venom for those who please God while those who rebel meet misfortune in her grasp.

What on earth must have marred God's beautiful creation in the woman, reducing her to a leftover; a relic of purpose by design? Surely, it must call for the intervention of heaven and a master plan of redemption to confront the chaos and restore creation to track, in the woman and her seed. However, there must be a definition of the chaos before deliverance of the creature and the creation can be effected.

*"And God made two great lights; the greater light to rule the day, and the lesser light to rule the night: he made the stars also.*

*And God set them in the firmament of the heaven to give light upon the earth, and to rule over the day and over the night, and to divide the light from the darkness; and God saw that it was good".*

**GEN. 1:16 – 18.**

In the creation of the cosmos, God made the stars also to function in a dual capacity: to give light upon the earth and to divide the light from the darkness; and God saw that it was good.

Perfect Adam, the arbiter of divine authority and perfection, was placed in this paradise of a Garden. The earth, covered with a vast firmament reaching both ends of the heavens and connecting the poles, was dotted with brilliant trinkets of stars.

Adam could turn his gaze to heaven above and appreciate it all but God was telling him in relative terms that these were symbolic of his seed to come, created to shine and give light upon the earth and to divide the light form the darkness.

Way down in the Genesis account, God made this relativity clear to Abraham.

*"And he brought him forth abroad, and said, look now toward heaven, and tell the stars, if thou be able to number them: and he said unto him, so shall thy seed be. By faith Abraham, when he was called to go out into a place, which he should after receive for an inheritance, obeyed; and he went out, not knowing whither he went. Therefore sprang there even of one, and him as good as dead, so many as the stars of the sky in multitude, and as the sand which is by the sea shore in numerable".*

**GEN. 15:5; HEB. 11:8, 12.**

Each star, symbolic of a seed, was all created to shine in the vast expanse of the heaven. No one star can hinder the shining of another star and, in the constellation, there are stars and there are superstars, for one star differ from another star in glory (1 COR. 15:41).

However, God knows the number of the stars and calls them all by their names and because He is mighty in power, Omnipotent, not one is missing (Psalm 147:4, 5; Isa. 40:26). The stars of heaven, in their multitude, reflect the seed of mankind in population on earth.

Before God set the stars of heaven in orbit, going back to the dateless past, there were a set of celestial stars known as **'morning stars'** and **'sons of God'** (GEN. 6:2; JOB. 1:6; 38:7).

These were angels and the chief of whom was Lucifer, son of the morning who, in the rebellion of pride, determined to exalt his throne above the stars of God and led a delegation of one third of the stars of heaven to rebel against God (**Isa. 14:12, 13; Rev. 12:4; 9:1**).

This led to their falling out of God's orbit and forming the graveyard of stars, reserved for everlasting darkness (**11 Peter 2:4; Jude 6**).

The serpent appeared in the garden at the verge of the birth of the human family, well before the woman brought forth her seed. These seeds were so important to God as they were created to shine and give light upon the earth, and to divide the light from the darkness: countless units of Adamic males covering the land and complemented with Adamic females for nourishment, fulfilling purpose. A master at deception, Satan stood at the threshold of vast humanity to reap a grim harvest of souls and perpetuate his diabolic agenda, in reversal to the divine purpose, on earth. This would be achieved primarily through the woman, by branding a trademark of sin on every seed born, he would multiply his stock of rebellion in humanity sparing no soul so long as it comes through the avenue of birth. Adam, the first man, had received this venom of sin polluting his blood and life, which transfers naturally to his seed after him.

*"And Adam was not deceived, but the woman being deceived was in the transgression".*

**1 TIMOTHY 2:14**

Rebellion is the stock in trade of sin and the satanic nature. SIN (the satanic nature) is the cause and curse, the virus, the venom of rebellion, and it became the undeniable, inescapable definition of the root of decay and death in the race of Adam. Using the negotiable instrument of the fruit of the tree of the knowledge of good and evil in the Garden, Satan has injected into the system and woven into the fabric and tissues of mankind's frame his venomous nature of rebellion,

Defiling, depreciating and negotiating God's purpose by design in the race of Adam. Adam and Eve's identity became corroded by sin and rebellion, which led them to hiding from the presence of God. Sin corrodes our identity and makes us to hide from God.

Sin is the lowest common denominator that brings all humanity to equilibrium. **'For all have sinned, and come short of the glory of God'** (**Rom. 3:23**).

However, in Jesus we find life, abundant life, and the life of God. **'In him was life; and the life was the light of men' (JOHN 1:4)**. The term life is the definition of identity, which being interpreted means that the identity of life, the individuality and uniqueness, is found in Jesus alone. Besides Him, we would struggle with an identity crisis and in the absence of identity, frustrations abound for man as well the woman. Sin is a sinker and sin will remove you from the scene, only if you flee can you be free.

Sin, the satanic nature, integrates into the system upon contact, takes root, and creates spiritual deformity, which leads to an identity crisis evident in our world today.

Satan, the great red dragon, inflicted with his tail of the satanic negotiation pact, drawing a great number of the stars of heaven, violating their purpose and deposing them from the orbit of God's firmament (Rev. 12:4). Sin brought a world of total darkness where the sun, in its full strength, cannot illuminate the soul or dispel the fear of the unknown future, a world where darkness, more dense than fog, could suffocate the soul.

*"And the dragon was wroth with the woman, and went to make war with the remnant of her seed, which kept the commandment of God and have the testimony of Jesus Christ.*

**REV. 12:17.**

The woman today is under attack. A satanic onslaught, tireless and unrelenting, is raging forever against the woman, violating her purpose, creating deflection, infecting every seed born and poisoning the man she was created to nourish, making her a stockbroker of the negotiation pact.

The woman is also God's agent in producing the seed that would crush the serpent's head and seeds that would enforce the verdict of Christ's judgement against the satanic violation and negotiation on mankind.

This chapter is dedicated to the mass of women: wives, mothers, ladies, daughters and girls, the female gender of the Adamic race; multitudes of women whose past (and present) bear the scar and sting of satanic violation and negotiation of their price and relevance as women.

The violated, the abused, the deprived and downtrodden, the relegated and neglected, and generally the negotiated in essence and presence; women reduced by sin to crack addicts, teen prostitutes, abused children, frightened wives. The curse has led to the clamor for protection, the cry, the confusion and the shame. Women the world over with poisoned minds, their bodies, the force of relativity, violated, their purpose defeated, their esteem crushed, their love corrupted and their essence dissipated. Reduced to a leftover, a caricature of the divine portrait, a relic of God's purpose by design, by a world so hostile to women.

The seed of man is infected with the venom of sin and rebellion. Immediately man fell and departed from the living God in rebellion, the religion they went into and the power that motivated them was witchcraft *'for rebellion is as the sin of witchcraft'* (1 Sam 15:23).

It is the universal religion of fallen humanity. Basically and fundamentally, witchcraft is rebellion against God's word and constituted authority, in heaven and on earth, for the earth is the LORD's and the fullness thereof. It is the spirit of compulsive manipulation sustained by sin. Spiritual witchcraft is the power of Satan, sustained and empowered by sin the satanic nature.

Congenitally, it is woven into the fabric and tissues of our lives, becoming our nature from birth. King Saul's action amounted to disobedience to God's command (1 Sam. 15: 18 – 24). His action relegated him to the realm of witchcraft. 'Righteousness exalts a nation but SIN is a reproach to any people' (Prov. 14:34). 'ANY PEOPLE' cuts across the color, geographical, cultural, and racial divide.

Lucifer is in a race against the woman. Skilfully orchestrated, he planned reaping the mass of humanity in all generation, planting a diabolic seed in every one born by the woman and multiplying satanic interests throughout the world.

God's pronouncement in the Garden, however, challenged the satanic agenda and changed the tide to divine triumph. The seed of the woman would crush the head (negotiation pact) of Satan and break the yoke over mankind (**Gen. 3:15**).

It is clear that things have gone wrong with God's original creation, cataclysms from which we now struggle to recover. Nevertheless, there is succour in the blood of redemption to wipe away the past, relatively and absolutely.

Through the power of the cross of Jesus and the blood of redemption, God's woman shall be redeemed and delivered from the compulsion to hide. Eve, alongside her husband, Adam, went into hiding in the aftermath of the rebellion and has reproduced generations of rebels playing hide and seek with God (Gen. 3:7-8). The game is up people.

The fig leaves of culture, tradition, legalism, education or other forms of aprons tailored to suit rebellion cannot cover the obvious spiritual nakedness in our world, or heal the hurts and violations that has marred our beautiful planet. God has prepared a new garden of hope, an haven called beginning again, where another chance to us is given to start anew, as yester pains and failures we bid adieu. A world pure and undefiled reserved in Zion.

It's in Jesus and the blood of redemption cleanses the past. The seed of the woman brought hope in Jesus. **HE CAME TO SET THE CAPTIVES FREE AND LEAD CAPTIVITY CAPTIVE.** The grey skies of sin, which created a fog that kept mankind groping in the dark, were dispelled when the star of Bethlehem arose, leading wise men to acknowledge Him as their king (Matt. 2:1-10).

The complexity and mystery of sin is beyond human comprehension and analysis and this is why God does not want us to understand His forgiveness but only to believe that He forgives sin.

It is only when we believe that our identity is restored in forgiveness and we are launched back to the orbit of God's purpose and fulfilment for us. When Jesus hung on the cross as the ultimate sacrifice for our sins, a cloud arose from the burning incense, which He represented, that spread around the world. It moved back through history to the beginning of man. It moved ahead from Calvary to that great day of His coming! As it spread through time and space, it covered ALL people of ALL ages who have placed their trust in the eternal COVERING, God's sacrifice of Jesus! A lost world has found its way as a result of the sacrifice of Jesus. God wants us to know that when He covers our sin, He covers it first so He can accept us, then He takes it ALL to a place where it can never be found. Our sins are not only covered, but they are removed **"as far as the east is from the west" (Psalm 103:12).**

The pains of the past can create a pain that last. Don't fight the pains. Labor pains are real and no matter how considerate and compassionate a doctor, midwife or the spouse of a woman can be, they cannot know the pangs of labor during childbirth save the woman alone. That pain, however, is the vehicle through which a miracle is born, a dream fulfilled, a prayer answered, the consummation of love delivered: **the birth of a child.** Pain is dreaded and avoided but pain can be used to produce a price that is not negotiable or transferable.

*"For we have not an high priest which cannot be touched with the feelings of our infirmities; but was in all points tempted like as we are, yet without sin"* **(Heb. 4:15).**

Christ bore the pangs of pain that was beyond human endurance to become our faithful High priest in God's presence.

*"Though he were a son, yet he learned obedience by the things which he suffered"* **(Heb. 5:8).**

*"Who, being in the form of God, thought it not robbery to be equal with God: But made himself of no reputation, and took upon him the form of a servant and was made in the likeness of men: And being found in fashion as a man, he humbled himself, and became obedient unto death, even the death of the cross.*

*Wherefore God also hath highly exalted him, and given him a name which is above every name: That at the name of Jesus every knee should bow, of things in heaven, and things in earth, and things under the earth;*

*And that every tongue should confess that Jesus Christ is Lord, to the glory of God the Father. And being made perfect, he became the author of eternal salvation unto all them that obey him".* **PHIL. 2:6-11; HEB. 5:9.**

Pain can be used to produce purpose and write a story complete and real. The pangs of Christ's atoning death produced an excellent glory of eternal impact on all who believe in His name.

That glory is not negotiable or transferable and we can only become as He is when we partake of the pain that attribute to His cause and purposes for our lives. *'For if we be dead with him, we shall also live with him. If we suffer, we shall also reign with him if we deny him, he also will deny us: if we believe not, yet he abideth faithful: he cannot deny himself'* **(2 Tim. 2:11-13).**

*For unto you it is given in the behalf of Christ, not only to believe on him, but also to suffer for his sake. For as the sufferings of Christ abound in us, so our consolation aboundeth by Christ. For our light affliction, which are but for a moment; worketh for us a far more exceeding and eternal weight of glory'* **(Phil. 1:29; I Cor 1: 5:4:17; Rom. 8:17).**

To rip through the dear and tender stuff of which life is made can never be anything but deeply painful. Yet that is what the cross did to Jesus and would do for anyone to be set free. The cross is rough and deadly, but it is effective. It does not keep its victim hanging there forever. There comes a moment when its work is finished and the suffering victim dies. After that is resurrection, glory and honour and the pain is forgotten for joy that we have entered in actual experience the presence of the living God.

The story of your life is like the writing of a book. The past episodes like chapters gone by. The end of a chapter does not determine or influence the tempo of the next. Each new chapter, however, is designed to bring the reader closer to the message of the story. The bleak and black episodes all combine to embellish and make the story complete and real; your story.

Your story cannot be complete without the bleak and black times in life when darkness hung over you; adverse episodes of abuse and violations when your lines became illegible and people could no longer read or understand your story.

Neither will it be real without these statements of subtraction. Times of deep seated emotional struggles when feelings betray faith, when practice violates principles, when conviction contends with the culture and courtesy of the world system (popular trend and opinion) around you.

The pangs of yester failures and pain eating away at your resolve to prevail in life and make a difference. However, using these as brushes of color, God, the master designer, embellishes our lives with His mercy and peace to write a story complete and real metaphorically called **'glory'**. Hebrews 2:10 give us a glimpse of this divine artistry.

The dark shadow of the past produces contradicting returns and creates the fear of tomorrow. These may all seem out of place, but through it all lines are formed, paragraphs are made, episodes emerge and chapters are developed; our lives eventually becomes a story, a combination of inconsistency, deficiency, and pain; the intricacy of daily existence woven into the fabric and tissues of life. God's editing makes all the difference for He makes all things- the irregular, illegible, illogical- blend and work together for our ultimate good and His eternal glory. Rejoice, He writes the last chapter… **you'll triumph!**

You will, in the name of Jesus Christ, finish your purpose. You will complete your mission. You will get to your destination. Your life will not be cut short in the midst of your years. God will not leave you stranded midstream. When He begins a thing He is faithful to complete it. You're still a work in progress. God is writing His eternal plan for you across a blackboard spanning your entire life. He has invested too much in you to stop the project. You are unique. You are real and complete in Him. You cannot waste His resources or call Him a liar; surely, the **Might of Israel** cannot lie.

There is a woman in you, a winner, a creator (of a home and happiness) a fulfiller (to a man) and a potential emancipator to your world. Waste not your tears and fret not over seeming fears. The divine pen is inked with blood greased from pain, rejection, sorrows and tears (Christ's and yours) to write a story complete and real; your redemption story. Our life stories become significant when through our relationship with Jesus Christ, they are woven into His story.

You will resurrect in triumph out of that pit of despair saith the LORD and soar with wings as eagle to heights of heavenly adventure, above the filth and decay of this world, where the air is fresh and clean. Reach out and touch the tangibility of His mercy and redemption in the blood through forgiveness of your sins.

Reach out in faith and be restored to the orbit of fulfilment and purpose by design in Jesus, as your womanhood is confirmed and your identity restored. You can be all you were created and empowered to be through the grace of redemption. Jesus only, through the grace of redemption, can give you a testimony, a reputation of integrity and value, and give credibility to your witness (Heb. 8:6). The blood has the answer and it speaks better things (Heb. 9:14; 12:24). That blood is empowered to deal with every defect of the sin virus congenital, endemic or pandemic, and restore that which the wild locust has eaten, the cankerworm has destroyed, and the caterpillar has devoured. It can turn your mess into a message, your tears into triumph, your deficiency to sufficiency, your trash into treasure, and give power to your witness. That blood can convert your violation to virtue again, your test to triumph, your turndown into turnover, your past to profit, your break up and breakdown into break through, your negotiation into appreciation and restore back your price that is not negotiable. **ALL THINGS work together for good to those who love God, to those who are called according to His purpose (Rom. 8:22).**

Jesus can turn the tides of favour and attraction back to your sail again and cause you to head towards the shore of fulfilment called home, where He waits with arms outstretched. There He has held your captivity captive and prepared gifts for the repentant of mankind.

For multiple hurts He offers multiple healings.

*'For this purpose the son of God was manifested, that he might destroy the works f the devil'* **(1 John 3:8). 'Woman, thou art loosed!' (Luke 13:12).**

In the final episode of the redemption story, God's orchestra will produce harmony in our lives as purpose and fulfilment embrace. A symphony composed by grand design, man and woman created and empowered, equipped with the seed and the womb.

**This, ultimately, is God's design for her fulfilment: the purpose of creation.**

*Panebi C. Smith*

# HER FULFILLMENT: The Purpose of Creation

*"And from Jesus Christ, who is the faithful witness, and the first begotten of the dead, and the Prince of the kings of the earth. Unto him that loved us, and washed us from our sins in his own blood, and hath made us kings and priests unto God and his father; to him be glory and dominion forever and ever. Amen.*

*'And I heard a loud voice saying in Heaven, 'Now is come salvation, and strength, and the kingdom of our God, and the power of his Christ: for the accuser of our brethren is cast down, and they overcame him by the blood of the lamb, and by the word of their testimony; and they loved not their lives unto the death'.*

*'Thou art worthy, Oh Lord, to receive glory and honor and power: for thou hast created all things, and for thy pleasure they are and were created'.*

*'Because the creature itself also shall be delivered from the bondage of corruption into the glorious liberty of the children of God. For we know that the whole creation groaneth and travaileth in pain together until now".*

**REVELATION 1:5,6; 12:10,11; 4:11; ROM. 8:21,22**

***"Thou art worthy, O Lord, to receive glory and honor and power: for thou hast created all things, and for thy pleasure they are and were created."*** **Rev. 4:11**

We have journeyed from sunrise in the dawn of creation to sunset in the close of the age. God's eternal worthiness will be revealed and acknowledged as all creation blends together to produce the pleasure of the most High in fulfillment to the purpose of creation.

God's eternal day is on the horizon of dawn. The Genesis account of creation projects it, while the Revelation series sums it up.

Man was made in the *image* of God, depicting personality and power, and in God's *likeness*, depicting perfection and purity. Empowered with divine authority as a great pulpiteer to lead the creatures' praise in creation's cathedral and, beyond this, to worship God in spirit and in truth. The woman, his companion, was created and endowed with God's essence, the divine attribute and character of mercy, beauty, purity and love. Empowered with God's presence and virtue to make a difference in a man's world and given a body, which formed the force of relatively, fashioned to minister to man's primary need of focus and nourishment.

The ultimate objective of the designer was the fulfillment of this design. **We were created for fulfillment, not by choice but by design**. The woman is so special to God. She was made an interface between God and man, a creature of purpose by design. A force of relativity, reflecting God's essence of beauty and mercy to the world of man, and a nourisher of man's mental and physical body and the medium of propagating man's seed on earth. Her destiny is encased in her definition, as a woman, her function, in womanhood, and her location in life-marriage.

She was created for fulfillment and only man is empowered to bring her fulfillment, not by choice but by design. Anything short of this will violate her purpose and negate her essence and worth.

A man's identity is enhanced by the conquest of his material and economic world, while the man she submits to as her husband influences a woman's identity. A woman's failure is tied to her inability to submit to a man in producing and raising a family but a man's failure is in his inability to provide economic security for his home and emotional security and fulfillment for his wife. The woman, made with the relativity of God's beauty and empowered to produce it in her seeds was deflected in purpose by Satan who, once full of wisdom and perfect in beauty, became corrupted with pride (**Ezek 28:12-17**). Violations now abound and captivity holds sway. The sexual delusion in our generation is appalling. The woman again stands a target of violation for two specific reasons.

Sexual intercourse is the medium of procreation and propagation of the seed of Adam, which replenishes the earth. Sexual intercourse is also as profound and impacting as worship, which produces a shield of security and welfare, derived from knowing the woman sexually, and the oneness of unity necessary to fulfill God's purpose of creation.

The sexual scourge has reached pandemic proportions in our time, destroying the seed of Adam through abortion, violating the purpose and relativity of the woman, and bringing sacrilege to the sanctuary of marriage and sex, which is sacred in relativity as worship. The sexual abuse run amok as victims of ritualistic sex abound; women violated by core Satanists in the occult that even when free from that association, still are paralysed by a vicious grip within, and captivated by demonic forces beyond themselves. Carried into relationship and marriage, these forces dictate the trend in the home, and in the nation, and multiply satanic interest on earth using women as multipliers and stockbrokers.

A definition crisis of womanhood looms today because the woman has been stripped of divine essence and presence, exposed to the insecurity of a failed shield of manhood, and reduced to a caricature of the divine portrait of womanhood.

Beaten blue and black in a world plagued by sin, using the instrument of violation, multitudes grope for identity and search for relevance as women. Something strange happened when Solomon, King of Israel, passed on and Rehoboam his son came on the scene.

Under King Solomon, God's people, Israel, had the greatest army that ever marched and the greatest people ever assembled.

For many glorious years he had reigned. Rehoboam was enthroned and he leaned on the arm of flesh instead of trusting in the God of his father, Solomon, and grandfather, David.

After five years of that foolishness, Israel had greatly deteriorated.

*"And it came to pass in the fifth year of King Rehoboam, That Shishak King of Egypt came up against Jerusalem: And he took away the treasures of the house of the LORD, And the treasures of the king's house; he even took away all: And he took away all the shields of gold, which Solomon had made. And king Rehoboam made in their stead brazen shields, and Committed them unto the hands of the chief of the guard, Which kept the door of the king's house".*

**I KINGS 14:25-27**

In the Bible, Egypt is always a picture of the world. With that in view, Shishak, the king of Egypt, is a picture of Satan, the prince of this world. Israel, under Rehoboam, had lost the power and the glory. The effectiveness of God's people was gone. So, Shishak came up and took away the treasures of the house of the LORD, and the treasures of the king's house ... *and he took away all the shields of gold which Solomon had made"*. The house of God and the king's house were invaded and emptied of its glory and relevance.

Man, basically and intrinsically, is the house of God made in the image and likeness of God. Symbolically, man's body serves as the temple of the living God **(I COR.3: 16,17; 6:15-17)**.

The woman, relatively, had a different function as she was fashioned to provide nourishment for the man chiefly in sexual intercourse and propagating his seed on earth. We also see outlined in Psalms 45 where the man is highlighted as king and the woman crowned queen, in marriage, and brought into the king's house;

depicting the home **(PSALMS 45:10-17)**. Further details in chapter 1, 4, and 7.

A shield is an article of war used to receive mortal blows. A shield is placed between the intended victim and the mortal enemy to take onto itself the blow that is intended for the destruction of the life of the victim. A shield does not merely ward off blow; it receives the blow instead of the victim and it, thereby, suffers damage and must be repaired if it is to remain useful.

In the design of the man, God has provided all the inherent capabilities to serve as the woman's shield. As a shield, God intends the man to be the source of physical security, economic security and emotional security for the woman.

Satan has come today to take away the treasures from God's people. Notice those golden shields in **verse 26:** *"He took away all the shields of gold which Solomon had made"*.

In 2 Chronicles 9:16, the Bible says, *"Three hundred shields made he of beaten gold"*.

Three hundred shekels of gold went into one shield. Those shields of gold were representative of the glory, the holiness, the power, and the greatness of Israel.

Now Shishak (the world and the Devil) has come and taken away those precious shields of gold. Rehoboam again displayed foolishness as, instead of calling on God for salvation and restoration, he commanded his servants to get brass and make brazen shields. He polished them up, set them up, then he grinned a deceptive smile and went right on acting as if nothing had happened. We have a picture here of what we have done in secular society and in fundamental Christianity. Specifically to the woman, the devil has come in and negotiated those shields of gold meant for her security, welfare and fulfillment, and violated her relativity and relevance that gives her a price. The divine presence and essence endowed on her, which gives her a price and her price is not negotiable, even the ornament of a meek and quiet spirit, which is in the sight of God of great price (I Peter 3:4).

In lieu of this, she has been given a false cover of brazen shields. Women rights movements abound today clamoring for equal rights with men, women emancipation, women empowerment and the likes but not women submission. The spirit of Jezebel is at work today and rampant in these last days. Foremost, it is the kind of spirit that makes ladies to reject authority. It is also the spirit that makes men to abdicate their roles and abandon their responsibilities. That spirit wears a religious garb and has infiltrated the church.

> *"Woe to the rebellious children, saith the LORD, that take counsel but not of me;*
> *and that cover with a covering, but not of my spirit, that they may add sin to sin:*
> *That walk to go down into Egypt, and have not asked at my mouth;*
> *to strengthen themselves in the strength of Pharaoh, and to trust in the shadow of Egypt!*
> *Therefore shall the strength of Pharaoh be your shame,*
> *And the trust in the shadow of Egypt your confusion".*
> **ISAIAH 30:1-3**

The familiar garb of culture and tradition and the covering of women right campaign that defies submission to God's command are not of God's spirit but of the world and they add sin to sin, rebellion to rebellion. The world today has traded the truth of God for the lie of Satan, satanic philosophy for the freedom in God's word, the tree of life for the knowledge of good and evil. The law of sin and death has replaced the liberty of the spirit of life in Christ Jesus.

A voice has echoed and reverberated through the ages down to our time. The voice of man in his fallen state,

> *"The woman whom thou gavest to be with me,*
> *She gave me of the tree, and I did eat".*
> **GENESIS. 3:12**

This insinuation and responsibility masking has kept man perpetually subjected to frustration and bondage of satanic deception. The deception cannot be further than that. By failing to see the true source of his opposition and recognize his primary assignment, he has been sidetracked to a mortal disadvantage, engaged in a war of attrition. Through the negotiable instrument of the fruit of the knowledge of good and evil, Satan has perfected the violation of the woman gender to the detriment of mankind.

Violations abound and the satanic negotiation on the lives of girls, daughters, and the woman in general goes unabated; the carnage, the depletion of divine substance and essence, which is relevant to complement the man's role in fulfilling his God-given task of dominating and replenishing the earth.

Satan knows that the pure knowledge of the woman, derived from the sanctuary of sex, is designed to produce a shield of protection, welfare and security form the man, a golden shield **(Gen. 4:1)**. Furthermore, that righteousness, holiness, power, and glory would be achieved in oneness and unity of spirit through married love and the consummation of sexual intercourse, producing an impact profound as worship, which creates oneness and unity with God. He has destroyed this arrangement by making the woman a sex symbol and arming the man with carnal knowledge, through ungodly and illicit sex, which has worked to the violation of women. Creating sexual abuse, social dislocation and relegation, the mental disrobing of her honor and dignity that is so rampant today; beyond these, the spiritual negation and compromise on her destiny and eternal relevance.

Outside God's arrangement the gold shields of righteousness, holiness, power, and glory in manhood, which guarantees protection and fulfillment of women in the permanence of marriage, is violated. Satan has replaced it, in lieu, with brazen shields of rebellion derived from sexual abuse and violation leading to insecurity among women. The gold shield represents the glory and is designed for the defense, protection and fulfillment of the woman in marriage. With the failure of the shield, the man is reduced to a state of inefficiency and resulting in multiple defects, especially in protecting the woman. Family ties become dead- no father, no structure, no order and no limits. Ironically, the woman's frustration has been in the area of her greatest need for fulfillment (according to design) and from the very one assigned to provide that fulfillment: **the man.**

In lieu of the golden shields they were created to be, men have been reduced to brazen shields by sin in disregarding and violating the sacredness of marriage and sex.

The woman, fleeced and insecure, now hides under the familiar cover of education, enlightenment and reforms parading under the guise of equal rights with men, women emancipation, women empowerment but not women submission as God designed and commanded for her fulfillment. Education, mental empowerment and knowledge, is a defense **(Ecc. 7:12)**. However, when it is used as a weapon against God's order of submission to the headship of a man in marriage, and blueprint for fulfillment, it becomes a false cover and is relative to trusting in the shadow of Egypt and leaning on the wisdom or strength of Pharaoh, which leads to confusion **(Isa. 30:1-3)**.

Recoiling in confusion, fear and insecurity, this has led to the clamor for rights and protection for women across the globe. Their near death life has pushed them to form alliances for jaded survival instincts, a sure sign of man's failure to provide a shield for the woman; the golden shield of holiness and righteousness in married love.

So long as God's law is being broken and violated regarding her salvation in marriage and childbearing as they continue in faith, love and holiness **(I Tim. 2:15)**, the negotiation of the woman and the dissipation of her purpose is sustained. The strength of the enemy is in the maintenance of ignorance. The Christian community, the body of Christ, the church, which has been empowered with unspeakable glory and manifold cure, has failed in challenging the limits and invasion of Satan, the prince of this world (symbolic of Shishak king of Egypt).

Satan is at work seducing Christians to speak what doesn't work where it doesn't matter. Rolling out messages that polish the brass instead of generating fire that refines and purifies men, making them golden shields of righteousness and glory. Our nation cannot hear us. The church is dismissed as a collection of escapists and relics. We are arranging deck chairs on a sinking ocean liner.

Just as the Philistines again reduced the people of Israel to a state of helplessness through a subtle means of disarmament, so the church has been stripped of power and glory through sin **(I Sam. 13:19-22).** No one wins a battle by manufacturing weapons on the battlefield.

The church is manufacturing weapons, programmes and activities that does not match fire for fire, while the enemy's onslaught against mankind rages. The woman, fleeced and abused, is subjected to the mercy of the uncircumcised Philistines in a world held captive by sin, the satanic nature. Congress is debating on sexual laws and reforms among teens while the torn and abused of our youth becomes a thorn in our flesh as we neglect and fail to embrace God's laws that transforms.

Nevertheless, God's woman shall be redeemed and restored to the orbit of fulfillment, not by choice but by design. God has provided nuggets for keeping the woman in orbit and maintaining her price. With these nuggets of truth in place, she is destined for fulfillment, not by choice but by design. Although feelings may betray faith, practice may violate principles and convictions may contend with the culture and the courtesy of the world's system around you, you can reach for the stars and stay in orbit.

## TIPS TO KEEPING YOUR PRICE

**SWIM UPSTREAM AGAINST THE TIDE:** Ocean tides and currents are so strong that they can stop or veer the navigation course of mighty ships. These natural forces wreak havoc on our environment and ecosystem. A similar tide flows in downstream human society and navigates society towards an end popularly accepted and embraced.

More sinister than nature, a great deal of these influence stems from ungodliness and works contrary to God's order and blueprint for human fulfillment. The combination of these influences has led to the counter productive results we see in society and in the home. We have moved one step forward and three steps backwards. The home has suffered from this sinister force, the nation has been affected and the church of Jesus Christ has been infected with its venom. A new generation of satanic negotiators has emerged on the scene. Empowered with satanic philosophy and doctrines of demons, they allure with persuasive words of man's wisdom, with fair speech and oratorical sagacity. They are pulling the crowds, the attention of the modern woman. Their doctrine of women empowerment is tailored to cover the woman with the garb of legalism, enlightenment, culture, and tradition that defies submission to authority and leadership of men, which violates fulfillment the purpose of creation.

Satan is again unleashing his familiar tool employed in the garden, the quest for equal supremacy with God's wisdom, and perfected in a wary world through the woman. Satan is attacking the fulfillment potential of submission each time the woman demands for equal rights with man. Beyond the subtle rebellion that frustrates fulfillment is a new generation of the seed of the woman being born and projected into a society saturated with filth and contradictions.

As a custodian of God's revelation of truth and purpose by design, you must swim against the tide upstream to embrace fulfillment. You were created and empowered to make a difference in the crowd of rebels and no force of opposition is potent enough to stop you.

> *"Associate yourselves, O ye people, and ye shall be broken in pieces; and give ear, all ye of far countries: gird yourselves, and ye shall be broken in pieces.*
> 
> *Take counsel together, and it shall come to nought; speak the Word, and it shall not stand: for God is with us.*
> 
> *For the LORD spake thus to me with a strong hand, and instructed me that I should not walk in the way of this people, saying,*
> 
> *Say ye not, A confederacy; neither fear ye their fear, nor be afraid.*
> 
> *Sanctify the LORD of hosts himself; and let him be your fear, and let him be your dread".*
> 
> **ISAIAH 8:9-13.**

The people of the world fear isolation and rejection and so, they form associations that empower their cause and secure their common interests. But the divine standard proves them wrong again and again and decrees that their end is doom. Your fulfillment potential as a woman is enhanced when you submit to God and make His healthy fear the objective in your heart as you swim upstream against the tide of societal norms, social accepts and national policies that contradicts God's blueprint for fulfillment, which is the purpose for creation.

**BE CONVINCED THAT YOU ARE NOT ALONE:** Loneliness creates vulnerability and exposure can show how insecure we truly are. However, with God you are not alone and cannot be left alone, you know. Association breeds unity; unity brings strength and forms a formidable barrier against opposition and external aggression. When people are united for evil, however, you may find them a force too strong to reckon with or oppose but God's decree is that though hand join in hand, the wicked shall not be unpunished **(Prov. 11:21).**

Elijah felt so lonely after the conquest of the prophets of Baal at mount Carmel. He had led a powerful revival session after which Jezebel the queen, wife of king Ahab, threatened his life. In loneliness and fear, he saw his vulnerability and complained to God but was rudely awakened by God's response.

*"Yet I have left me seven thousand in Israel, all the knees which have not bowed unto Baal, and every mouth which hath not kissed him".*

**I KINGS 19:18.**

God had kept a reserve that had not negotiated their price with the negotiable instrument of Baal worship. Scattered across the land were units of God's faithful holding forth the banner of righteousness and the promises of God in a polluted world. God's reserves are in the land today and they are not alone. Beneath the stress, the trials, the tears, the frustration and set back, the intricacies of daily existence; life's stretching, making us inelastic, confused and depressed lies **the everlasting arms**, bearing the weight of His creation, you and I inclusive.

**The Omnipresent eye,** maintaining equilibrium in the universe. **The omniscient mind** that knows the pains we bear and willing to share. The omnipotent assurance that you are NOT ALONE in your earthly sojourn and cannot be left alone, for He has said, *I will never leave you nor forsake you*"(**Heb. 13:5**). You are not alone and cannot be left alone and the acceptance of this assurance in your struggles can make the difference between giving up and going on, between hope and despair, between life and death and between heaven and hell. *"Lo, I am with you always, even unto the end of the world"* (**Matt. 28:20**). You are not alone!

*And a man shall be as an hiding place from the wind, and a covert from the tempest; as rivers of water in a dry place, as the shadow of a great rock in a weary land.*

**ISAIAH 32:2**

For that lonely woman out there, God has someone, a man, specifically designed and assigned to you. He has your specifics with him and he is closer to you than you imagine. He is not a spirit but his definition is spiritual. He came from God, the Father of all spirits, and his true identity is linked back to God's purpose and presence where he is fully defined and empowered to function.

This function, relatively and absolutely, will lead to your fulfillment as a woman and meet the purpose of your creation. Ultimately, God will be glorified in the creation when man and woman attain fulfillment in function as purposed and ordained by God.

For the pure and undefiled girls out there who have not bowed to the Baal worship of rebellious sex but have kept their garments unspotted, their price not negotiated, their essence and worth intact; despite color, creed, race, religion or tradition, God's man for you is on the way. He is on divine assignment to bring fulfillment to your fondest dreams. Beyond the divide of the common and average, he will take you to heights of mental, physical and emotional fulfillment and pleasure. He will be the sunshine in your hair, the shadow on your ground, the beat in your heart; the moonlight shinning down, the whisper in the wind and he will always be there for you.

He is not a superman neither is he going to be a perfect being. He is God's word of assurance to you made flesh and relative to your need and your body, which you have preserved in holy estate and purity for him will be the force of relativity and priceless gift of bonding you to him, mentally and emotionally, for life. You have been divinely equipped to bring equilibrium to his world and he will reach to that body for affirmation at all times.

Beyond your every imagination, you will marvel at the revelation of love as God purposed it in marriage. You body is the container of this divine agenda of love and life and it is imperative that you co-operate with God by keeping it pure and undefiled till marriage if you must receive the fullness of His purpose, which is your ultimate fulfillment.

## BE CONVINCED THAT THE END WILL WELL WORTH THE EFFORT:

The woman was taken out of man but her definition and fulfillment, the two most important functions, were left in the man. A woman, basically and intrinsically, owes her definition and fulfillment to a man not by choice but by design. The divine design spells her definition as woman, her function as womanhood, and her fulfillment as marriage, for only in marriage can her womanhood and fulfillment attain perspective and man only is empowered to create this. The modern philosophy of women liberation and emancipation from men and the family violates the family structure and dissipates God's purpose by design. A woman can be successful in life's ventures, which includes education, entertainment and business, but only in uniting with a man in marriage and building a home, irrespective of the fruit of children, can she attain fulfillment, not by choice but by design. God's hierarchy of authority and leadership spells that the husband is the head of the wife and the home as Christ is the head of the man and the church. The recognition of and submission to this design works to produce fulfillment both for the home and the church. For the home is a prototype of the church.

The doctrine of equal rights with men, championed by women, violates submission to God's hierarchy of leadership and headship, which brings fulfillment to the home and the nation. Women empowerment entails giving the woman the right to education, enlightenment, and a voice in her world. But the equal rights syndrome is congenitally defective as it orientates the woman to view the man as a competitive partner in a competitive world and not as the head and fulfiller in a world programmed for fulfillment through obedience to God's commands. Our being made in the image and essence of God makes us all joint heirs of the grace of life **(I Peter 3:7)**, but only in obedience to God's command and submission to His order of fulfillment can our prayers be answered. Equal rights and attitudes may sound trendy but the divine design proves them wrong. The world today has developed a standard of right standing but the divine design proves them wrong because they lack divine life. God's way of life for us is not known by external indications but by divine registrations. It is only that which issues from God's life that forms Christian conduct; therefore, we cannot consent to any lifestyle that does not spring from life. *The power of the Holy Spirit combines with the word of God in the execution of the Christian way of life producing a lifestyle, in us, that will meet with divine approval.* Choosing to obey God rather than the order of the day is the key to change, for human life has been programmed for fulfillment through obedience.

Reason tells us there is a God. Design speaks and says that there must be a Designer. Creation declares that there must be a Creator. Effect demands that there is a cause. Nature shows God as a creator of beauty and infinite variety. Thus portraying that there is a better way of existence; a world of new frontiers and ever expanding discoveries reserved for mankind, revealed only through willful inclination to God's way of life. Obedience to God's commands ushers into a new way of life, a new mind with new desires, and new insights for living producing new results. And with this renewed mind comes the power to face every challenge that come our way in life **(Heb. 5:8,9)**. This little dot of time in eternity is our brief opportunity to learn how to be OBEDIENT to God when everything around us says "Disobey!"

The only things that will be sustained by the power of God are those things that are ordained by God, started by God, and operate in obedience to God. God ordained marriage from the onset of time. Marriage was not man's idea. It is from the beginning to the end a divine phenomenon. It must begin and end with God. Anything outside the divine triangle of God, your spouse, and you violates purpose and evades fulfillment. But the puzzle becomes solved when we comply with the revelation and definition of the Maker in obedience.

**Perfect obedience would be perfect happiness if only we have perfect confidence in the power we are obeying.** The end will be worth the effort of obedience to God, be convinced. One reason why you are a woman is because God made you so.

You are a peculiar creation, a unique being, and a rare combination of God's matchless grace. God's species of purpose by design fashioned in His likeness and made in His own image. Circumstances cannot change you otherwise, ethics and tradition cannot improve on God's design; color, creed or racial difference does not determine your destiny, culture or calling cannot influence it. Neither can philosophies nor enlightenment guarantee fulfillment. What determines your productivity and reward is obedience to God's blueprint of purpose by design revealed in the Bible, God's word.

You don't clamor for rights; you have been created and endowed with right by reason of your design and empowerment of your essence. Lots of women are crushed in their esteem, downcast in their role, relegated in their position and defeated in their purpose because they lack understanding of God's purpose by design for their fulfillment. They suffer from an identity crisis. Your true definition is in God's word. You must go beyond yourself to discover purpose and source for divine information to fulfill destiny. Go beyond the surface, dig deep, search for purpose, quest for relevance and cry for meaning.

Your change shall come and you will make a difference when you search with all your heart.

Across the divide of the common and average lies a destiny beyond your imagination, glorious and complete, acquired only through that ardent desire to prevail in life and make a difference. You are not a means to an end but an end in itself and the end will be well worth the effort when you walk in obedience to God's commands.

**BE CONVINCED THAT YOU WILL REPRODUCE GENERATIONS AFTER YOUR KIND – GOOD OR EVIL:**

Something very sophisticated evil and powerful, unrelenting is conspiring to get you to accept a deadly substitute for your destiny. This monster seeks to make you live symbolically instead of actually, relatively to God's purpose for your life instead of absolutely; to have a form of godliness' but denying the power of it **(2 Tim. 3:5)**. Living dead people are everywhere. At some point their dreams, visions and zeal were extinguished, and a lower form of living began. Their body language reveals them. God's word is explicit about reproducing after our kind whether good or evil.

*"And God said, let the earth bring forth the living creature after his kind, cattle, and creeping thing, and beast of the earth after his kind: and it was so.*
*And God made the beast of the earth after his kind, and cattle after their kind, and everything that creepeth upon the earth after his kind: and God saw that it was good".*
**GEN. 1:24.25**

God ensures that we reproduce after our kind basically and intrinsically, symbolically and essentially, relatively and absolutely, whether it is good or evil. *One damaged temple cannot destroy a century of tradition but one weak link can break the chain of a mighty dynasty.*

The human family is the mightiest dynasty on earth but one weak link in Eve, through sin and rebellion, brought violation and negotiation to the human family per head. *"All have sinned and come short of the glory of God"* **(Rom. 3:23)**. No one stands alone and every human failure, or victory, resonates far beyond our comprehension even to generations to come.

Sin is a sinker and sin will remove you from the scene; only if you flee can you be free.

Sin is no respecter of color, culture or religion; it afflicts all and violates the divine agenda for your life, frustrating God's purpose and plans through the power of your wilful choice and reproduces your kind naturally. Sin fascinates then it assassinates. It thrills but then it kills, and if you play you pay.

*I do not frustrate the grace of God!* Paul the Apostle reverently charged **(Gal. 2:21)**.

You can frustrate the grace of God by your willful choice to linger in rebellion but be assured that you will reproduce after your kind. You cannot frustrate the grace of God and escape, God cannot be mocked; your action attracts divine reaction and your seed determines your harvest **(Gal. 6:7,8)**. The works of the flesh listed in **I Corinthians 6:9-10** and **Galatians 5:19-21** are negotiable instruments powered by the negotiation pact of Satan against mankind. Each of these negotiable instruments listed in scripture dissipates God's purpose for your life and violates the divine essence endowed on you. However, sexual immorality is the chief denominator and highest common factor in negotiating your price. For every sin or negotiable instrument employed is activated outside of the body but sex intrudes into the inner court, the holy of holies, and brings sacrilege to God's embodiment of purpose; the force of relativity to man of God's essence of beauty and purity, your body.

By negotiating sex, you corrupt your body with the spirit of harlotry, dissipate your essence downstream and you destroy your relativity to man and God outrightly. You impeach the divine credibility in your life. Your womanhood and its capacity to be fulfilled are handed over to the destroyer and come under manipulation in basic and fundamental ways.

Completely taken over, darkness sets in, your growth rescinds to a halt and the depreciation begins. Multitudes are held hostage in a valley of decision, the lost of Adam's race, of the daughters of Eve; destiny denied, purpose defeated, bodies violated and price negotiated. The negotiation and frustration knows no bound while the stink reach high heavens.

Many women are plunging into marriage headlong and hitting the hard bottom. Most ladies reject authority and carry that spirit and attitude right into marriage. When the divine essence endowed on a woman is destroyed how can she protect a man's focus, which she is empowered to do, when she doesn't know what it is? How can she reduce distractions when she becomes the greatest source of distractions? And how can she create the dream environment when she has never been subject to authority in any environment? She will only reproduce after her kind – rebels!

## BE CONVINCED YOU WERE CREATED FOR FULFILLMENT, NOT BY CHOICE BUT BY DESIGN.

You were created for fulfilment, not by choice but by design. The proper functioning of your body is designed to produce efficiency, which leads to productive living. The eye dictates your view; the ears discern sounds and your brain interpret them. The legs move your body away from danger too fast for you to make a choice. Your body works independent of your choice to produce efficiency and fruitfulness and God works through your mind and will to do His good pleasure in your life **(Phil. 2:13)**. Either ways you gravitate towards His purpose for your life and ultimate creation, which is fulfilment. Your fulfilment goes beyond your choice to meet your design.

Your choice says, if all things work out fine, I will be fulfilled. Design speaks and says, *"all things work together for good to them that love God"* **(Rom. 8:28)**.

Choice says, "I wish I was born abroad, in a better country! Design speaks that *"the earth is the LORD'S and the fullness thereof"* **(Psalm 24:1)**. Choice says, "I wish I were never raped and abused in the past". Design thunders *"for this purpose was the Son of God manifested, that he might destroy the works of the devil and, Behold, I make all things new ... for the former things have passed away"* **(I John 3:8; Rev. 21:4,5)**.

Choice says, "I wish I were a man, if only I had strength like a man". Design declares, *"A virtuous woman is a crown to her husband; strength and honor are her clothing"*
**(Prov. 12:14; 31:25)**. Choice says, "I demand equal rights with man". Design speaks solemnly, *"For the man is not of the woman; but the woman of the man. Neither was the man created for the woman; but the woman for the man. For the husband is the head of the wife, even as Christ is the head of the church: and he is the Savior of the body"*. **(I Cor. 11:8,9; Eph. 5:23)**. Choice says, "I am contented and fulfilled as a woman, I don't need a man".

Design declares, *"For the LORD has created a new thing in the earth, a woman shall compass a man"* **(Jer. 31:22)**. Choice says, "I wish I were a beautiful and elegant woman".

Design declares, *"The king's daughter is all glorious within: her clothing is of wrought gold; even the ornament of a meek and quiet spirit, which is in the sight of God of great price".* **(Psalm 45:13; I Peter 3:4).**

Your destiny must be not be mortgaged. Your hand in marriage is not for the highest bidder. Your price is not negotiable; it must be paid in full. Whatsoever man that you offer privileges of your body without commitment and divine approval in marriage negotiates your price. You carry a price tag and it is not for the highest bidder.

You were created for fulfillment, not by choice but by design. Even if your choice in being fulfilled has been corroded by episodes of violation and abuse that have marred your past, or you have been relegated to the background by lack of education and enlightenment, reduced to a social relic in a changing world. Your case might be that sin and rebellion have deformed you, making you a caricature of the divine portrait of a woman, reduced to a leftover in a world void of God. Through God's empowerment and grace endowed on you by reason of your purpose and design, you can still reach for fulfillment. The blood of Christ entails that you can be bought back to purpose. The blood is God's negotiable instrument and buy-back of your purpose for creation. Your choice of repentance will bring God's intervention and restoration of your essence and your design as a woman ensures your fulfillment. You can make a difference in a man's world. You can be restored back to orbit again. You can still rise above the filth and decay of this world to heights of heavenly adventure where the air is fresh and clean. You can be restored back to orbit and shine in the firmament of fulfillment that you were created and empowered to be.

The virgin birth, immaculate life, sacrificial death and triumphant resurrection of Jesus Christ, the seed of the woman, ensures the fulfillment of your purpose and guarantees your comeback. Your fulfillment is the purpose of your being created, not by choice but by design. You are the passion of a man's life and the force in his world.

As a woman you may want to isolate yourself from all that has been said in this book. You may even see yourself in a different setting other than God's woman as portrayed in this book. This, however, does not change the fact that you are a woman- God's woman.

**One reason why you are a woman is because God made you so and so you remain.**

If you will then accept this unchangeable fact and surrender to God's purpose unconditionally, only then will you attain fulfillment and peace, not as the world gives but as Jesus gives and provides. If you isolate yourself in rebellion, you will find yourself entangled in the web of frustration, caught in the cycle of satanic negotiation and manipulation. Satan's grip on humanity is firm and he has a stake hold in your life naturally from birth, despite your color, your persuasion or religion. Your natural birth subjects you to his manipulation and as a tool, he exploits your existence to his advantage; your very life and daily existence he uses to promulgate his interests on earth. Your living becomes a cycle of his manipulation, which leads to frustration **(Gen. 6:5,11,12; Jer. 17:19; I Tim. 2:14)**. Only the blood of Jesus, God's negotiable instrument in the seed of the woman, can break the power of negotiation and satanic cycle of manipulation and frustration, which begun in Eden but has covered the face of the earth, reproduced in every seed of man born by the woman.

Your failure is not rooted in societal decay and neither is your defect connected to your background; *the whole world lies in wickedness* **(I John 5:19),** nor is it tied to a partner who has abused and violated your person in the past. Your failure springs from the root of your rebellion to God's purpose for your life revealed through God's commands, which works for your ultimate fulfillment. This congenital defect is connected to the failure of Adam and Eve, rooted in rebellion and reproduced in mankind through childbirth.

We are born into a satanic order and victims by nature. Born into a hapless, hopeless and helpless situation. Apparently, everything has gone wrong with God's order, cataclysms from which we now suffer, not from God's side of the divide but from man's dimension on earth. God designed that the ultimate fulfillment of the woman would be in marriage so he made the man first, empowered him with the capacity of welfare and security in the Garden of Eden, before creating the woman. Significantly, she was not made as an after-thought but God wanted man to see the need for a female companion, as displayed in the creation, and her relativity to him. And not until man gained the perspective of divine relativity was she made and brought to him; this gave her a worth and a price that was not negotiable. Together, under God, they formed the first human family unit on earth, a replica of the spiritual church that had been born through Christ before the foundation of the world.

God showed His great love for the family when He formed the family before the church on earth. The garden was God's 'nest' where the first family would share their relationship and raise their seed. Though they missed it through sin and rebellion, God did not leave them there, in His mercy He went before them to raise a seed that would restore back the purpose for the family and the fulfillment of creation.

That seed, Jesus our LORD, brought sanity and restoration back to the life and home of man. Beginning in Eden, He made the home as a model of the church and all related levels of ministry. Our capacity to minister is developed in the home where God's tools are sharpest and the heat is the greatest. We can only flourish in ministry when we have received the seed planted in the garden of the home. Just as a red blood cell carries life–sustaining oxygen to every part of the body, the family is the transport that allows us to deliver the gospel in basic and fundamental ways that otherwise may not be possible.

In the middle of this configuration lies the woman, created and endowed with God's presence and essence; a rare combination of God's matchless grace, brought forth and made relative to man. God's force of relativity in teaching man of His eternal unconditional love and mercy, revealed in the woman. Ordained as a member of and empowered to complement and fulfill the most sacred and intimate of human relationship, marriage, which consist of two, the woman's role cannot be overemphasized. Strategically placed between God and man, she was to reflect the character and beauty of the omnipotent God, otherwise clouded or unknown to man, and act as a circuit breaker in nourishing the man, reducing distractions and streamlining him to focus on the objective of God's assignment for him.

Created equal in spiritual essence yet different in presence and function. While the man tends to the garden and dresses it, the woman provides the booster to keep him going strong and focused. The woman was made God's cushion-effect to man that as he labors, he can find comfort in a place called home and as well build a wall of security and welfare around that comfort zone.

For this function, God gave her a **body,** which became the force of relativity to the man.

Wherein contained all the intricacies of purpose by design making her complete and real. In that body was a **nakedness,** which formed the beauty of suspense in the man, **virginity** necessary to bond her to the man spiritually and emotionally for life. A **sexual** complement was she made, as a gushing fountain head, to nourish the man and quench his deep seated thirst for passion and intimacy; a soul provender.

To crown it, she was empowered with **love**, God's fruit of Agape, which gave her the power of unconditional choice and acceptance of the man even when dreams do not come true, when expectations fail, when desires are not granted, when the puzzle of life does not fit and the overwhelming evidences are odd; she sticks to him in faith and trust and her heart goes on to love and cherish him. A product of this love was **passion,** which inspires her in all she does within and outside the perimeter of the home but for the advancement and fulfillment of the man. While the man builds the house (his domain or empire), she builds the home (the cradle of his affection and reward for his conquest) in raising his seed.

A complementary strength of **beauty** in the inner man was given her, even the ornament of a meek and quiet spirit, *which is in the sight of God of great price* (I Peter 3:1-4).

Coupled with this was **virtue,** God's endowment of power on the woman, which made her a crown to the man and gave her a price far above rubies, a price not negotiable **(Prov. 12:14; 31:10).** Finally, she was given an elastic soul capacity to **grow** so long as she was appreciated and her role duly recognized and honored in the man's world. When the level of appreciation runs low, depreciation sets in and the spirit begins to wither.

***Indeed, her creation is an epitome of appreciation and no other instrument can be employed to activate her growth.*** The serpent brought sin's violation to this perfect configuration of man and woman, the home and family, and spilling over to the church and the nation but God's decree brought restoration and redemption through Jesus Christ our LORD, the seed of the woman. This ensured that God's plan for eternity, the past and future, and which brought forth time in the middle will be fulfilled and this was the purpose of creation. She is fully restored through the blood, God's negotiable instrument in buying back sin-deformed creation, and redeemed; created to create purpose in union with man.

A new generation of women is emerging on the scene. They are intelligent, exuberant and precocious. It's a new ball game all together entirely. Basic biblical accepts are being put to test while social norms are being challenged. Universally acknowledged terms like "women are the weaker vessel" now demand explanation by the social reformers. "The man is the head of the house" is no longer automatic. It is now being redefined and subjected to proofs in the crucible of modern challenges and demands, practice not just theory. Men now have to sit up, work extra hard, and develop their minds, brains, personality and spirituality. The trouser alone is no longer the proof of manhood. Biological characteristics are no longer enough. The stakes have been raised. The ladies have increased the **"cut-off"** mark for manhood.

But in all God's woman is being revived as a new generation of men is being raised.

Men empowered as golden shields to bring definition and fulfillment to women. They are waking up from their slumber and developing themselves spiritually, mentally, physically, financially and emotionally. They are being blown out of the catacombs of oppression, irresponsibility, violation, abuse and relegation of women, and bringing them to the forefront of appreciation and recognition of their roles as helpers in the great harvest of replenishing the earth and restoring the lost glory of the family, the nation and the church. Together we are marching unto the shore of fulfillment where God's purpose in the making of the home, the nation, the church and consequential to the creation of the woman, is fulfilled, not by choice but by design.

From the cities, towns and villages of nations they will emerge, to lead a triumphant return to righteousness as the home is restored, the nation redeemed and the woman's purpose and essence realized. She will be launched back to God's orbit of fulfillment as she bears seeds that carry divine credibility, virtue and calling; seeds empowered to perpetuate Christ's bruising of Satan's head and negotiation pact on mankind. We shall see it and be glad, the impact covering the land as the waters cover the sea. God's will be done on earth as it is in heaven. Hastening the return of our Savior and LORD, Jesus Christ, in relativity to the woman's fulfillment, the purpose of creation. You shall be fulfilled, not by choice but by design, in Jesus' name!

You are sure to happen, woman, sooner or later, it will surely come, it will not tarry wait for it; your happening.

God's garden shall be restored, devoid of the serpent's presence but beautified with the woman's essence. She was created and endowed with God's essence and presence, and empowered to make a difference in a man's world. This gives her a price and her price is not negotiable.

Woman thou art loosed!!!

# Epilogue: ANSWERS FROM THE FATHER'S HEART

Ministry basically means affecting lives; affecting lives, creating impact, raising the standard; the effect, the impact, the standard. **The Effect** speaks of the capacity to produce a change, a definite clause of purpose in the lives of people. **The Impact** is the result, the force of change, the tangible result of contact and the word becoming flesh in material and realistic proportions. **The Standard** refers to God's way of life and answer for mankind. He alone sets the precepts and defines the terms for us, for human life has been programmed for fulfillment through obedience. God has an answer for man encoded in the effect of His Word. The Impact of this word is released through obedience, when God's Word and Spirit are released to work in us to produce a lifestyle that will meet with divine approval; internal indication producing external registrations. God creates an effect on the inside that registers an impact on the outside.

This is the standard of God for man. Ministry becomes the effect, the impact, the standard encoded in God's answer for man. God has an answer for you. Answers to challenge the limits and the opposition in your life and force them to a retreat. Answers to heal your hurts and mend your broken heart. Answers to deal with your frustration and fear, and equip you to return fire for fire for the enemy's onslaught. Answers to light the darkness and enlighten our confused world.

Log on to Answers @ ***God's Word*** and download results for your life. Answers that can give you that needed turnover in your marriage, your business and your ministry. Answers that will turn loose your vision and give your dream a quantum leap from survival to significance, from recess to excess, from conception and carriage to tangible delivery. Answers that will convert your testimony from story to glory give your life a reputation of integrity and value and give credibility to your witness.

The odds are overwhelming, people. The tides are high and the current so strong; you must swim upstream against the tide if you must prevail and make a difference. There is a sinister force that has arrayed itself against you; a satanic contract taken on you to defeat your purpose, frustrate your mission, mortgage your destiny, negotiate your price and stop you from happening. You were created with a fighting spirit, empowered with divine strength and equipped with the armor of God. You must rise up and confront that enemy, oppose your opposition, stop that stopper, defeat the negotiator, kill your fear and frustrations and return fire for fire till the foe is vanquished in Jesus name.

You must go beyond yourself to discover purpose and source for divine information to fulfill your destiny. This is contained in the Bible, God's Answer, where your true definition is found. Go beyond the surface; dig deep and search for purpose, quest for relevance and cry for meaning. Your change shall come and you will make a difference when you search with all your heart. You are sure to happen, sooner or later, it will surely come, and it will not tarry: your happening.

Across the divide of the common and average lies a destiny beyond your imagination, glorious and complete; acquired only through that passionate desire to prevail in life and make a difference... recovered only when discovered.

**ANSWERS FROM THE FATHER'S HEART** is all we need and when you have answers your price is not negotiable.

Something hidden! Go and find it. Go look behind the Ranges Something lost behind the Ranges. Lost and waiting for you. Go for it and be blessed.

# ABOUT THE AUTHOR

**PANEBI CHURCHILL SMITH** is a dynamic young man born for a time like these. Born on November 24, 1975, he was raised by a godly mother and groomed by two role models of Pentecostal ministers, Revs J. O. Doroh and Sunday Umukoro. Growing up in Lagos, Nigeria, West Africa, and a onetime Youth President of Divine Christian Assembly, a thriving Pentecostal church with headquarters in Lagos, his life is one marked with divine providence and encounters.

A man with a rare combination of God's matchless grace, he has received the requisite hue of the spirit.

**"ANSWERS FROM THE FATHER'S HEART'** is Churchill's peculiar ministry to the body of Christ. He says "when you have answers your price is not negotiable and God has equipped each one of us with answers for our confused world"

He is married to Malisa and they make their home in Virginia Beach, Virginia. Speaking of his wife he calls, "an answer to my quest for companionship, my inspiration, and her price is not negotiable!"

He serves his country on active duty in the United States Navy. Expect more answers in his books.

Author contact- ebi25ng@yahoo.com.